"Judaism is fluid, dynar
Each generation needs te
ity for its time. David Lieberman is one of these teachers, and his
Transcendental Judaism is a beautiful expression of what Judaism
can be. This is not an easy read, but it is a rewarding one."

—**RAMI SHAPIRO**, author of *Judaism Without Tribalism*

"*Transcendental Judaism* presents us with some familiar teachings,
but David Lieberman's unique interpretation ties them together in
a compelling, integrated, and practical manner with profound implications for a better world. This book is a must-read for all who
want to learn how Judaism can be a transformative force in their
intellectual and spiritual journeys. It is a theological guide that is
rooted in the past but paves a dynamic new path forward."

—**SHMULY YANKLOWITZ**, president
and dean, Valley Beit Midrash

"Bravo! *Transcendental Judaism* offers a wise and accessible guide
to Jewish mystical practice. Lieberman clearly is a seasoned Jewish
teacher and practitioner whose insights are rooted in decades of
serious study and experience. For anyone seeking a deeper understanding of Judaism's mystical and transcendent pathways, I highly
recommend this book."

—**ESTELLE FRANKEL**, author of *Sacred Therapy*

"Rooted in the fertile soil of traditional and mystical Jewish texts,
Transcendental Judaism envisions a new (yet ancient) kind of
spirituality. Each of us can hear God's 'still, small voice' and attune
ourselves to it. Thereby we become more centered and balanced,
able to begin to mend ourselves and our society."

—**DANIEL MATT**, author of *The Essential Kabbalah*

"*Transcendental Judaism* combines a personal story of spiritual opening with a theology based on contemporary readings of Jewish mystical teachings. It is a book written by a layman, speaking directly and unpretentiously about truths he has learned over a lifetime of meditation and study. Well worth reading! Give it a try."

—**ARTHUR GREEN**, author of *The Heart of the Matter: Studies in Jewish Mysticism and Theology*

Transcendental Judaism

Transcendental Judaism

Enlivening the Eternal Within to
Uplift Ourselves and Our World

David L. Lieberman

RESOURCE *Publications* · Eugene, Oregon

TRANSCENDENTAL JUDAISM
Enlivening the Eternal Within to Uplift Ourselves and Our World

Resource Publications
An Imprint of Wipf and Stock Publishers
199 W. 8th Ave., Suite 3
Eugene, OR 97401

www.wipfandstock.com

PAPERBACK ISBN: 978-1-6667-5864-1
HARDCOVER ISBN: 978-1-6667-5865-8
EBOOK ISBN: 978-1-6667-5866-5

02/01/23

To my teacher who awakened my Jewish soul and provided a road map to guide me through the richness of our Jewish texts.

Maimonides . . . taught that animal sacrifices were only commanded to the Jewish people as a concession because it was the only type of Divine worship known in that era; it was progress from the pagan standard of human sacrifice. He also taught that prayer was evolution from animal sacrifice and a more silent meditative type of worship will eventually supersede prayer with words.

—RABBI DR. SHMULY YANKLOWITZ,
Existing Eternally, Existing Tomorrow

Contents

Preface

THIS BOOK WAS WRITTEN during volatile times. We have been living in the midst of a worldwide pandemic. Economic and social inequalities have strained the fabric of our society. Weather anomalies—rising temperatures, along with hurricanes and floods—have been occurring with unprecedented frequency and severity. Around the world, the schism between the political left and the political right has been growing wider.

Yet we persevere and move forward, attempting to fashion a world that reflects our belief systems and values. Many of us struggle to secure food, clothing, shelter, safety, and basic health necessities. Others have the luxury of being able to reexamine our careers and priorities. All of us strive for respect, dignity, meaning, and love.

For Jews, does a connection with God factor into our lives? Whether we are religiously observant or not, many of us are looking for a palpable connection with God, or with a higher spiritual power. How do we find and make that connection? Some of us choose to dive deep into the commandments, finding direction and meaning from them. Others of us see the commandments as anachronistic, a throwback to a primitive time. In this case, it still makes sense to give to charity, refrain from stealing, and repent the wrongs we have done, but only from the standpoint of a secular ethics.

For many, God and religion have negative connotations. God is "too ethereal to understand," "unresponsive," or even "nonexistent." Religion is "too dogmatic," "out of touch with modern life," or "totally irrelevant." For many of us who are asking the big questions in life, it is safer these days to say, "I'm spiritual, not religious."

But what if those two terms, "spiritual" and "religious," were not mutually exclusive? What if we could recognize that our mystical and traditional texts use different language to convey messages that are consistent, complementary, and applicable to our lives in eminently practical ways? For example, both our mystical and our traditional texts teach that everything in the universe emanates from a single source of infinite intelligence and potential for creativity. Traditionally, Jews call that source "God." We are made in the image of God; that is our essence, it is never beyond our reach. When our awareness touches that source, we enliven its infinite capacity in our lives and, simultaneously, uplift ourselves and the world around us.

Each of us receives and assimilates Jewish teachings in our own way. Our individual backgrounds, experiences, and beliefs inform how we do so. Of course, our understanding is not static; we change and grow. Talmud teaches that "one who reviews his studies one hundred times is not comparable to one who reviews his studies one hundred and one times" (b. Ḥag. 9b).

Therefore, I invite you to join me in taking another look, to review our studies for the hundred-and-first time. My hope is that this book will provide some new and inclusive perspectives on our sacred writings, and indeed on our lives.

Some Notes on Wording and Gender

Throughout this book, for grammatical ease and readability, I use the term "God." For those who are more comfortable with the concept of a "higher spiritual power," please indulge me; I believe we are talking about the same thing. And for those who object to the spelling out of G-d's name, I ask you to please forgive me. In my attempt to reach a diverse audience, I have had to make some difficult and imperfect choices.

I have also chosen not to refer to God as "He" (except briefly when I talk about the stereotypical "bearded man on a throne above the clouds"), and in quoting scriptures or other sources, I usually have modified the male pronouns "He/Him/His" to "God/God's."

Also, when speaking generally of a person or people, scriptures often uses "he/his" or "man/men." In most cases, I have changed the wording to "one/their" or "person/people." If you see one of these words above written in brackets, for example [God], that mean that the original source from which I am quoting probably said "He/Him/His" or "G-d."

Speaking of gender, you may also notice that most of the rabbis and other authorities quoted from centuries past are men. That is the nature of the traditions that have been handed down. In the twentieth and twenty-first centuries, on the other hand, we do have many women who have thought, written, and published on these matters, and they are among the many experts cited here.

Acknowledgments

THANKS TO MIRANDA NADEL for introducing me to Torah study. Thanks to Rabbi Dr. Shmuly Yanklowitz for his reviews, suggestions, and encouragement to continue. Thanks to Rabbi Jonathan Magidovitch for his insights and perspectives. Thanks to Rabbi Jonah Rank for his early work researching text sources for me. And thanks to Rabbi Rami Shapiro and Professor Adam Chodorow for their review and feedback as this book was beginning to take shape. I thank Rabbi John Linder for asking me to share "My Jewish Journey" with our congregation; that talk became the introduction to this book. Thanks to Professor Daniel Matt for his Zohar classes and for reviewing my bibliography and recommending additional sources with which I needed to become familiar. Over the years, the weekly Torah commentaries of Dr. Robert Rabinoff have been an inspiration to me. I am grateful to Rabbi David Levinsky, Professor Evan Finkelstein, and Rabbi Alan Green for their insights and suggestions, and to Rebecca Glenn for coaching me over the finish line of the manuscript. I thank Anna Geller for her guidance and my skillful editor, Marie Deer, for improving the clarity of my writing. I offer deep gratitude to my oncologist, Dr. Michael S. Gordon, who assists me to conquer chaos and is an anchor during turbulent times.

I am grateful for all of the help of many kinds that was given to me by the people named here, but all opinions expressed here are my own and any errors or omissions are my own responsibility, not theirs.

Abbreviations and Transliterations

Hebrew Bible

IN THIS BOOK, WHEN I refer to the Bible, I am referring to the Hebrew Bible, known as the Tanakh. Tanakh is an acronym for the three major sections of the bible (Torah—the books of Genesis through Deuteronomy, Nevi'im meaning Prophets, and Ketuvim meaning Writings). Christians often refer to the Hebrew Bible as the "Old Testament."

Unless otherwise cited, quotations used from the Hebrew Bible are taken from the website of Sefaria, Inc., www.sefaria.org.

I use the following abbreviations in referencing the books of the bible, though not every book is referenced in this work:

Torah		Nevi'im—Prophets		Ketuvim—Writings	
Gen	Genesis	Josh	Joshua	Ps or Pss (pl)	Psalms
Exod	Exodus	Judg	Judges	Prov	Proverbs
Lev	Leviticus	1–2 Sam	I & II Samuel	Job	Job
Num	Numbers	1–2 Kgs	I & II Kings	Song	Song of Songs
Deut	Deuteronomy	Isa	Isaiah	Ruth	Ruth
		Jer	Jeremiah	Lam	Lamentations
		Ezek	Ezekiel	Eccl	Ecclesiastes
		Hos	Hosea	Esth	Esther
		Joel	Joel	Dan	Daniel

Torah	Nevi'im—Prophets		Ketuvim—Writings	
	Amos	Amos	Ezra	Ezra
	Obad	Obadiah	Neh	Nehemiah
	Jonah	Jonah	1–2 Chr	I & II Chronicles
	Mic	Micah		
	Nah	Nahum		
	Hab	Habakkuk		
	Zeph	Zephaniah		
	Hag	Haggai		
	Zech	Zechariah		
	Mal	Malachi		

Mishnah and Talmud

All references to Talmud are the Babylonian Talmud, abbreviated "b."

I use the following abbreviations in referencing tractates/chapters in the Mishnah and Talmud. I only list abbreviations for those tractates/chapters I use in this work:

Mishnah		Talmud	
ʾAbot	Pirkei Avot	B. Meṣ	Bava Metziʾa
		Ḥag.	Hagigah
		Nid.	Niddah
		Pesaḥ.	Pesahim
		Sanh.	Sanhedrin
		Šabb.	Shabbat

Transliterations of Hebrew Spellings

For ease of reading, I do not use the Hebrew alphabet in this book. When I occasionally spell out Hebrew words, I use English transliterations. For example, in spelling out one name of God, I write YHVH which are the Hebrew letters *Yod Hey Vav Hey*. Transliterated Hebrew words can be spelled differently in English, depending upon the source or author. Some authors use dashes: Y-H-V-H. For consistency, following are examples of spellings I use throughout the book regardless of the spelling in the source I quote.

Assiyah, Yetzirah, Beriyah, and **Atzilut**—the four supernal universes experienced by Ezekiel when he saw the chariot (*merkava*): made, formed, created, my glory.

Ein Sof—"without end" in Hebrew. Sometimes spelled *"Ayn Sof," "En-Sof," "Eyn Sof,"* or even *"Ein-Soph"*, with or without dashes.

Mitzvah (sing.)/**Mitzvot** (plural)—the 613 commandments in the Torah. Sometimes spelled *mitsvah/mitsvot*.

Nefesh, ruach, neshama, chaya/yechidah—the four levels of the soul.

Pshat, Remez, Drash, Sod—the four levels through which we study and interpret Torah: the plain meaning, the allegorical connection, the homiletical lesson, the mystical interpretation.

Sefirah *(sing.)* /**Sefirot** *(plural)*—the ten inner qualities of God: *Keter, Chochmah, Binah, Chesed, Din/Gevurah, Tif'eret, Netzach, Hod, Yesod, Malchut/Shechinah*.

Zelophehad—the father who had five daughters: *Mahlah, Noah, Hoglah, Milcah,* and *Tirzah*, who challenged God's laws of inheritance.

As above, if you see one of these translations above written in brackets, for example [*Ein Sof*], that mean that the original source from which I am quoting used one of its other spellings.

Introduction

IT'S APRIL 5, 1975, a gorgeous spring afternoon in St. Louis. Sitting comfortably in an overstuffed chair, I am experiencing a sense of peaceful calm I have never known before. The window is open, and my awareness turns from within; my ears reengage. The following thought is seared into my brain: "The birds in the trees and the cars on the highway are singing the song of life together in perfect harmony, and the world is unfolding just as it should be."

As I was emerging from my first-ever meditation session, this was the very first thought that I had.[1] As I had been told it would, my mind's awareness had shifted from manifest reality (that which is "out there") to the un-manifest: pure awareness, the place from which everything springs, the place of nothingness and, at the same time, of infinite possibilities. In Judaism we call this the *Ein Sof* ("without end"). And with my awareness now shifting back out to the manifest, my mind was automatically applying my experience of transcendental unity to the objects that hit my attention in everyday existence. In other words, I was spontaneously integrating the qualities of the *Ein Sof* into my everyday life.

• • •

1. I meditated using the technique of Transcendental Meditation° . Information about it can be found at www.tm.org.

Introduction

I do want to make a brief but important detour here. When someone says "the world is unfolding just as it should be," many of us think, "Are you kidding me? No it's not! Just look around: that's why we perform acts of *tikkun olam* (repair of the world). We've got to fix all the things that are broken in this world." And that is true; *both* statements are true at the same time. The interplay between what is happening at this moment in the world and what could happen in the next moment, based upon the actions (both individual and collective) that we undertake, is a whole different discussion, and one in which I will not go into depth in this book.[2] Instead, what I'm sharing with you here is my own, direct experience: when God's grandeur touches me, the overriding message is the perfection of God's handiwork.

• • •

Now that I've told you how powerful that very first experience was for me, you will probably not be surprised to learn that I've been meditating regularly ever since, for almost fifty years now. And I want to describe for you how this repeated experience of that "still small voice," the voice that Elijah heard (1 Kgs 19:12), the voice that says nothing and everything at the same time, has affected my life, has made Judaism come alive for me, and has given me a sense of our ability to connect with God.

In the aftermath of the terrorist attacks of September 11, 2001, the economy took a dive, and I was laid off by my employer of twenty years. After watching me do some extensive thrashing around, my wife correctly figured that she had better take matters into her own hands, and suggested that we take the kids and the dog and go live in Mexico for a while. (Friends of a friend had done that and they loved it.) Having little else to offer at the time, I agreed, and, after renting out our home in Phoenix and putting my severance money in the bank, we landed in San Miguel de Allende, a small, beautiful town full of cobblestoned streets in the high desert of

2. See Artson, "God of Becoming and Relationship," 11–12. I come back to Rabbi Artson's book, which introduces the reader to Process Theology from a Jewish perspective, in chapter 6.

central Mexico, a town with a lot of art and culture and a long history of visitors from the United States. And of course, a synagogue. We enrolled the kids in school and I started studying Spanish and Torah. There was a weekly Torah study group. I became enthralled. After a while, instead of just showing up, I would go online in advance and read the weekly *parsha*. (The Torah is divided into weekly portions, so that the entire Torah is read over the course of the year; Jews all over the world read the same portion, called a *parsha*, every week). A little while after that, in addition to the *parsha* itself, I was also reading several commentaries about it in advance of the study group each week.

San Miguel opened our eyes to a new culture. People are warm, the pace of life is slower; things get done when they get done. (One of our early jokes: What time does this store open? Answer: When the shopkeeper arrives! And somehow, that turns out to be just at the right time.) Our kids, aged three and eleven when we arrived, became fluent in Spanish within a few months. San Miguel is a walking town; you run into your friends while doing errands throughout the day. We stayed on for a second year, but with high school approaching for our older daughter, we made the difficult decision to return to the United States. I soon found a job in my field, and continued to pursue more reading, group study, and individual study of Torah. That reading and study eventually led me to a course in Mussar, a centuries-old Jewish practice in character development and spiritual growth. I then entered a multiyear training program to become a spiritual director, so that I would be able to accompany others on their own spiritual journeys.

Then, a couple of years later, something strange started to happen. As I would read and study Torah, the words, which for many years had been interesting intellectual concepts to me, began to come alive. They started to jump off the page as though they had a reality, a life of their own.

For example (Gen 12:1–2), when God says to Abram (the name by which Abraham was known at that time) *Lech L'cha*, telling him to leave behind everything he knows and that God will show him a great place and will bless him, these were no longer just words on paper to me. I actually experienced that. Leave behind the life that I knew so well. What is that life? It is the life of thoughts, of objects, of activities and emotions. Leave it behind and God will bless me with something more ... a direct experience of God's quiet existence: no thoughts, no activity of the senses, just the powerful, peaceful experience of pure awareness.

When Jacob, on his way to find a wife, dreams of a ladder with God's angels ascending and descending on it and receives God's assurances that God will guard him and be with him always, and then wakes up and says, "Surely YHVH is present in this place and I did not know it!" (Gen 28:16)—Jacob is talking directly to me. He is saying, "I might not have always realized it in the past, but God is always here—always available to me wherever I am—and always will be." What does "available here ... and available now" mean? It means, as the Hasidic rabbi known as the Kotzker Rebbe (Menachem Mendel of Kotzk, Poland, 1787–1859) said, that "God resides wherever we let God in."[3] And I actually experience that; at any time or place, I can simply be quiet, and God will come in. God is always there ... it's just that in those moments, God seems to move from the background to the foreground—and then afterwards, unfortunately, God moves to the background again.

But is it really an either/or situation? The sages of various traditions talk about having an awareness of God's presence within them at *all* times. In Judaism, we refer to this as *devekut*—as "cleaving" or "attaching" to God. In Deuteronomy, Moses gives this advice to the Israelites: "by loving the Lord your God YHVH, heeding God's commandments, and holding fast to God ... thereby you shall have life, and shall long endure" (Deut 30:20).

Rabbi Abraham Joshua Heschel (1907–1972), an influential theologian and civil rights activist, writes about this experience in his essay "An Analysis of Piety":

> Piety is thus a mode of living. It is the orientation of
> human inwardness toward the holy. It is a predominant

---

3. Cooper, *God Is a Verb*, 69. Cooper is citing the Kotzker Rebbe via Kaplan, *The Chasidic Masters*, 186; Cooper also refers to Wiesel, *Souls on Fire*, 175–93.

interest in the ultimate value of all acts and feelings and thoughts. With his heart open to and attracted by some spiritual gravitation, the pious man moves, as it were, toward the center of a universal stillness, and his conscience is so placed as to listen to the voice of God.[4]

What if all of us were able to have that sense of universal stillness—and not just when we are sitting quietly (although that's not a bad start), but while we are going about our daily lives? What if we could have a palpable sense that we could always hear and follow God's silent voice?

Then how would we treat the stranger, the oppressed, the widow, and the orphan?[5] And what about our own family members? Would we spend our days or conduct our business differently? Might charity, repentance, prayer, and repairing the world—*tzedakah, teshuvah, tefilah,* and *tikkun olam*—take on new meanings for us? What might the world be like if God's transcendent presence were to become lively in our everyday awareness and permeate our every thought, feeling, and action? My experience is that *this* is what Judaism is asking us to pursue.

4. Heschel, *Moral Grandeur and Spiritual Audacity*, 308.

5. On the ethical treatment of the stranger, the widow, and the orphan, see, for example, Exod 22:21, Deut 14:29, and Deut 26:12.

Chapter 1

What Is Transcendental Judaism and Why Does It Matter?

ALMOST FOUR THOUSAND YEARS ago, Abraham forged a radical new path for Western theology. He sensed the presence of a singular God, transcendent and incorporeal, yet one with whom he made a personal connection. His life was transformed. Over the millennia and day by day, Jews have yearned to do the same. Through the giving of Torah, the commandments (the *mitzvot*— from the Aramaic root *tzavta* meaning attachment or connection[1]) have provided us with ways to bring us closer to God.

For some of us, strict adherence to the *mitzvot* as traditionally practiced provides an immanent sense of connection with God. For others, not so much. Can the rest of us find ways to practice the *mitzvot* (make the connection) that *do* give us a sense of awe, that help us become aware that we are part of a larger cosmos around us? We can—through the meditative quieting of the mind that lets us directly experience the transcendental nature of God, which is also our own essential nature. Our sages have done this in

---

1. Freeman, "What Is a Mitzvah?", lines 15–18. Thanks to Rabbi Alan Green for bringing this to my attention.

the past. Both our traditional and our mystical texts tell us that not only do we have the ability to align and unify ourselves with God, it is our mandate to do so. Furthermore, the implications of doing so on a regular basis are life-changing, not only for ourselves but for our society. Our texts tell us that if we walk in God's ways and cleave to God, there will be better days ahead.

Let us, then, explore the Jewish journey of connection and examine how, without abandoning our current practices, we can revitalize ancient practices and expand the ways in which we can enliven the eternal within us. If we take the initiative to regularly *experience* the "still small voice"—not just to think, feel, or talk about it—we can integrate God's qualities of infinite intelligence and creativity into our daily thoughts and actions. Our lives will become richer. Let us seize the opportunity to bend the arc of history and help usher in a new era, to follow on the eras of biblical Judaism and rabbinic Judaism—a new era that I call transcendental Judaism.

The Era of Biblical Judaism

The time period from God's covenant with Abraham until the year 70 CE is known as biblical Judaism. This early step in our journey included the receipt of a written teaching, the *Torah*, describing the relationship between God and the children of Abraham. The Torah contains, among other things, 613 commandments, or *mitzvot,* that specify right actions, both positive and negative, for the people to follow. More than a hundred of these commandments address the Temple, sacred objects, and sacrifices and offerings to God.[2] The root of the Hebrew word for "sacrifice," *korban,* also includes meanings of "approach" or "come close." It was through these sacrifices that Abraham's children could come closer to God by acknowledging God, praising God, and asking God to expiate their sins. At that time in human development, sacrificing to gods was a meaningful way of coming closer to a power that people felt was bigger than

2. Rich, "613 Mitzvot," #426–#560.

themselves. Along with the practice of the other *mitzvot*, these sacrificial practices continued until the year 70 CE, when, in response to an unsuccessful Jewish revolt against Roman rule in Jerusalem, the second Temple was destroyed by the Roman Empire.

The Era of Rabbinic Judaism

After the Temple, where the sacrifices had been performed, was destroyed, and millions of Jews were killed or dispersed, Jewish practices had to evolve. Over the next several hundred years, our sages and scholars actively developed the oral law, or *Mishna*, as an extension of the Torah, and, around the year 200 CE, the rabbi called Judah the Prince assembled these teachings and wrote them down. Later, commentary on the oral law, or *Gemara*, was also compiled and transcribed. The *Mishna* and *Gemara* together, along with other commentaries that were added over the years (including the medieval commentaries, or *Tosafot*, and those of Rabbi Shlomo Itzhaki—Rashi, 1040–1105), comprise the present-day Talmud, one of Judaism's major great works.

In addition to the Talmud, Jewish law has been rich in many other writings to help us better imagine, understand, and internalize God and God's teachings. These include the Zohar, Judaism's mystical commentary on the Torah; the Shulchan Aruch, a codification of Jewish law; the vast writings of Rabbi Moshe ben Maimon, or Maimonides (1138–1204), the great medieval Sephardic philosopher; and others far too numerous to list here. Denominations such as Reform, Conservative, and Reconstructionist Judaism, as well as the Hasidic and Renewal movements, have emerged to establish communities and practices through which we can live Jewish lives in ways that are meaningful to us. Mussar is a way of study and practice to grow our spirituality and deepen our ethics.

And finally, at the core of this great expansion in both depth and breadth that has become our Jewish heritage over the last 3,500 years, there remains the practice of the *mitzvot*—including study (*limmud*), prayer (*tefilah*), acts of charity (*tzedakah*), and repentance (*teshuvah*)—which helps bring us closer to God.[3]

The Era of Transcendental Judaism

Beginning with Abraham and continuing with Moses, other prophets, rabbis, and modern-day seekers and mystics, the Jewish people have a history of connecting personally with God. Abraham and Moses took detailed instructions directly from God. Other prophets had occasional visions, dreams, and/or transcendental experiences. Some of us feel God's presence in prayer, at the birth of a child, at the bedside of a sick friend, watching a sunset, or simply while washing the dishes. What does God's presence feel like? It is often a pervasive sense of peace, calm, knowing, shimmering, or oneness with one's surroundings. For many of us, these experiences are fleeting and seem to arrive (and, sadly, depart) randomly. But if we are fortunate enough to have had such a deep experience at least once, it often makes an indelible mark on our lives.

Surprisingly, as unusual as this kind of experience seems, it also feels perfectly natural and right. And because we are not used to describing it in words, many of us may not tell anyone about such an experience for years. We might vaguely wonder what the experience was, where it came from, what it meant, whether it had anything to do with Judaism, and perhaps, if we are bold, how we can make it happen again. This ability to *make it happen again*— the regular, reliable, repeatable practice of directly experiencing the infinite transcendental nature of God, of *Ein Sof*, through the meditative quieting of the mind, and then bringing that back out into the world through our thoughts and actions—is what I am calling "transcendental Judaism."

3. As Talmud teaches: "Shimon the Righteous . . . used to say: the world stands upon three things: the Torah, the Temple service, and the practice of acts of piety" (`Abot 1:2).

Continuing the Performance of the *Mitzvot*

Might I be suggesting that in the future Jews will be transcending through meditation, but will no longer perform the *mitzvot* as we currently understand them? For many reasons, I am not saying that at all.

First, the practice of the *mitzvot* will continue because they are at the core of Judaism. The *mitzvot* are the commandments we received from God on Mount Sinai (or, if your belief is less traditional, given to us by the sages) and they define our relationship and covenant with God. They guide us in life by specifying which actions conform to God's will and which do not. And we operate according to the axiom that actions that conform to God's will are "right actions": vehicles for making us better people and for making the world a better place for all.

Second, transcending is not done simply for its own sake. Transcending immerses us in a direct experience of God's infinite nature, which we then carry into our everyday activities. Our task, one of our *mitzvot* (which I will discuss further below), is to cleave to God,[4] to carry a sense of God's presence with us in whatever we do.

Third, the sacrifices that were made during biblical times and the study, prayer, acts of charity, and repentance of our rabbinic times are *representative* acts that define and reflect the collective spiritual maturation level of the Jewish people at each of these times. Sacrifices were prominent, but they weren't the *only* thing our ancestors did to come close to God; they performed the other *mitzvot* as well. Similarly, studying, praying, and performing acts of charity and repentance are prominent today in our rabbinic times, but they are not the *only* things we do now to come closer to God; we perform the other *mitzvot* as well. And likewise, in the future, the process of transcending through meditation will not be the *only* thing our children and grandchildren will do to come

---

4. Deut 10:20: "You must revere YHVH: only your God shall you worship, to [God] shall you hold fast, and by God's name shall you swear."

closer to God; they, like their ancestors, will continue to perform the other *mitzvot* as well.

Our journey is a long, evolutionary one during which our pathways for connecting with God gradually become more numerous and, perhaps, more sublime. As we move forward, we are not burning the bridges that previously connected us with God; instead, we simply continue to build additional ones in order to broaden and enhance our paths of connection.[5]

Will the *Mitzvot* Evolve?

I am not trying here to sidestep the important debate over whether the *mitzvot* will evolve over time; I view that as a different topic than the theme of this book. Whether or not the *mitzvot* will evolve is a debate over whether ours is a "perfect Torah" (*Torah Emet*, literally "true Torah") or an "evolving Torah" (*Torah Chayim*, literally "living Torah"). *Torah Emet* teaches that

> the commandments and the conventional halacha [laws] are as perfect as they can be, and that no halachic changes can be made concerning the commandments, even when they appear to be unjust and are not compatible with the moral spirit of the age.[6]

Torah Chayim, on the other hand, teaches that

> Torah was given at a particular moment in time, and as such, while completely divine, often expresses ideas and commandments which were a compromise to human weakness (i.e. sacrifices and the permission to own slaves). These laws must be seen as "Torah tolerated" rather than as "ideal" Torah laws. As such, the Sages of Israel were not only permitted to, but in fact *obligated* to "update" the Torah to higher, more ideal standards,

---

5. On the question of whether we will also restart the practice of animal sacrifice, see chapter 6.

6. Cardozo, "Perfect Torah—part 2," para. 4.

depending on the moral and religious conditions of their days.[7]

I happen to believe that ours is a *Torah Chayim*, a living, evolving Torah, but that is *not* my basis for arguing that we can accomplish a connection with God in multiple ways and on multiple levels. As we will discuss in greater detail in chapter 3, we understand and connect with Torah and the *mitzvot* at four levels: with the plain or literal meaning (*pshat*); through a hint or an allusion that we sense (*remez*); by means of an explanation or an interpretation that we understand (*drash*); and at the mystical level (*sod*). We are used to our *mitzvot* touching us at the levels of our bodies (*pshat*), our hearts (*remez*), and our minds (*drash*). Why not also connect at the ethereal or transcendental level (*sod*), especially if we can do so effectively and reliably?

Is Transcending Really a Jewish Idea?

This idea that all of us have the ability to directly experience the transcendent, the source from which everything springs . . . in other words, God—is this really a Jewish idea? Absolutely!

- **The notion of one single incorporeal God, one source of creation:** this concept, this monotheism, is the story of Judaism itself.

- **The notion that connecting with that source is within our grasp:** Torah tells us that we are created in the image of God (*b'tzelem Elohim*, Gen 1:27), and that the spark of that divinity resides within all of us.

- **The notion that we have a desire to connect with that source:** this is the yearning expressed throughout all of our texts, from Torah, through the rest of the Bible, to Talmud and the Zohar: we yearn to cleave unto God, to walk in God's way, to have God's light shine upon us.

---

7. Cardozo, "Perfect Torah—part 2," para. 5.

- **The notion that we can and must take action to accomplish that desire**: this, too, is a consistent message within our tradition, which makes it clear that it is up to us to respond to God's invitation to connect. We have made, and will continue to make, efforts to follow God's many commandments. In biblical times, the actions we took included animal sacrifices. In our current rabbinic times, study, prayer, acts of charity, and repentance are key components of our efforts. And now, we have the opportunity to enter a new era. Meditation, the act of quieting the mind to directly experience God's transcendental nature, and of bringing that into our daily lives, is our next, additional response to God's invitation to us.

- **The notion and practice of meditation**: this practice has deep roots in Jewish life and tradition. The act of meditation, as a way to transcend and connect with God, is not new. The rich history of meditation may well be as old as humankind. In the Western world, it has gone somewhat underground in the last few hundred years, thought to be relevant only to the most pious, but it has begun to resurge and become more mainstream in the last thirty to sixty years. In chapter 4, we will briefly recap what modern-day rabbis have uncovered about the practice and spread of Jewish meditation. This is an ongoing exploration; I do not believe we have fully tapped its secrets.

But What's Wrong with the Way We Currently Practice the *Mitzvot*?

Why would we want to connect with God differently? Doesn't the regular performance of study, prayer, acts of charity and assistance to others, repentance, and the rest of the *mitzvot already* invoke a connection? Indeed it does, for some of us, more so than others. But what I am suggesting is that in the era of transcendental Judaism, we can add to our repertoire of ways to enliven our connection with God.

In the introduction to this book, I described my experience of such a connection. And for almost fifty years now, I have had the good fortune to repeatedly experience what Heschel described as a "universal stillness." Accordingly, my other connections with God have felt significantly less profound in comparison.

Think, for example, of your own experience in prayer. I will describe mine. Prayer is, after all, intended to be direct communication with God. At the best of times, that is what it is. But in my experience, sometimes the words come out mechanically, and the prayer is over before I have even realized I am reciting it. Sometimes I don't even say the words myself, but listen to the rabbi, cantor, or congregation, while my mind wanders, thinking of . . . yes, God, but also about all the things that fill a mind, like whether I am going to go to the gym later or let it slide, what I need at the grocery store, or if I need to find another citation in order to reinforce a particular point in this book. Sometimes, I do actually say the words with *kavanah* (intention), contemplating their meaning and being emotionally moved by their power. But am I ever taken beyond myself to experience, as Heschel describes, "a universal stillness" through prayer? It may have happened, but I can't say for sure. Clearly, others may experience prayer differently, may be more present in the moment and with God. In my own experience, though, I find that it does not truly and reliably connect me to God in the way that I would want.

And what about the act of preparing Thanksgiving dinner at the synagogue to give to the homeless? It feels good, I can't deny that . . . I may even make a new connection with a fellow congregant. And the experience would probably feel even stronger if I were regularly serving the food directly to the person in need. For others who fully immerse themselves in intense acts of charity, I have no doubt that the experience is very powerful. But again, from my own experience, I can only say: although it feels good, it does not move me strongly; it does not forcefully connect me with God.

And other *mitzvot*? Leading the Seder at Passover, returning the extra dollar bill mistakenly handed to me in change, reading *parsha* commentaries and discussing them at Torah study each week: performing these and other *mitzvot* is good. It is certainly better than *not* performing them. I will acknowledge that there is some satisfaction involved in all of these activities. But I find that no matter how intensely I perform these *mitzvot*, what I experience is never as profound as the experience of direct immersion in God's transcendental nature, which then fills me as I go back out to engage with the world.

It is not far-fetched to assert that we can have direct experience of the "still small voice" and the ability to enliven its qualities in our lives. As I will demonstrate throughout this book, our tradition teaches that everything in creation is nothing but the manifestation of our unseen God. We are all aspects of the infinite intelligence, creativity, and possibilities of the universe. Our sages tried to bring that reality from the background to the forefront of their awareness because doing so would align their lives with it. Our texts and modern research reveal that the benefits of doing so are measurable, tangible, and real—both for ourselves individually and for our society.

These teachings are not new. I am simply presenting them from a new perspective, using modern terminology. I hope to make it clear that our ability to live spiritually elevated lives is not a long-lost hope buried in a jumble of ancient-sounding words. Let us accept the teachings and wisdom of our sages as real and understand that we can make them relevant in our lives today. Let us experience new old ways to connect with God. Then, fueled and energized with the power of creation itself within us, let us engage in life full-on, bringing the bright light of God's love, mercy, and justice to ourselves, our families, and our communities.

Chapter 2

The Quest for the Transcendent in Jewish Texts

God, the *Ein Sof*, and the *Sefirot*

Let's start with the impossible: defining what we mean by God. In the introductory sections of this book, I have used the terms "God" and "*Ein Sof*" interchangeably. But what do these terms mean, and do they refer to the same or different things? You will probably not be surprised to hear that there is no agreement among Jewish sages and scholars on the answer to that question.

In Judaism, we have dozens of names for God. I will mention only a few of these names here, and very briefly describe their attributes; following that, I will go into greater detail about the *Ein Sof*.

God

From the bearded man sitting on a throne in heaven to the brilliant sunset falling below the horizon, and everything in between—these are our concepts of God. God is the creator, the judge, the merciful, the One who loves unequivocally, the wrathful One, and/or the one who doesn't exist at all. God is in heaven, holy and separate from us—or God is the spark inside each of us. God transcends the universe, surrounds it, fills it, or all the above.

YHVH

"*YHVH*" (the Hebrew letters: *Yod Hey Vav Hey*), the Tetragrammaton, is the name used most frequently in the Bible to refer to God. This name is typically pronounced as "*Yod Hey Vav Hey,*" "*Adonai,*" "*Ya,*" or "*HaShem*" (which means "The Name"), and a common translation is "Lord." (Speaking the full name aloud was permitted only to the High Priest in the Temple on the day of Atonement, and that pronunciation is currently lost.) The name "*YHVH*" denotes eternal existence and carries the attributes of lovingkindness, awe, and mercy.[1]

Elohim

"*Elohim,*" actually a plural word used in the Bible to refer to princes, judges, and even other gods, is translated simply as "God." This name is used when emphasizing God's might or creative power (e.g., in creating the world in Gen 1:1). "*Elohim*" carries the attributes of justice and rulership.[2]

Shechinah

The "*Shechinah*" represents God's divine presence on earth. At the start of Shabbat, when we begin to feel closer to God, we welcome the *Shechinah* as "God's bride," and we sing *Lecha Dodi*, "Come my Beloved." The *Shechinah* represents the connection of God in heaven with God on earth, the uniting of the transcendent with the immanent.[3]

---

1. Werblowsky and Wigoder, *Encyclopedia of the Jewish Religion*, 160; Rich, "Name of G-D," para. 7; Cooper, *God Is a Verb*, 71.

2. Werblowsky and Wigoder, *Encyclopedia of the Jewish Religion*, 160; Rich, "Name of G-D," para. 8.

3. Citron, "Lecha Dodi Prayer."

Ehyeh Asher Ehyeh

At the burning bush, when Moses asked God what God's name was, so that Moses could convey this to the people, this is the answer that God gave: *"Ehyeh Asher Ehyeh,"* which translates as "I Shall Be As I Shall Be" (or "I Will Be What I Will Be"; Exod 3:14). This name conveys an infinite sense of just "being"... across all time. It also conveys the notion of a dynamic God, a God with whom we have an ongoing, interdependent relationship[4]—because the future is left unspecified. This name has profound implications for the understanding of a God who is, as we will explore in chapters 3 and 6, the spark that is the essence of "being" within each of us.

The *Ein Sof*

The term *Ein Sof* (literally "without end") does not appear in the Bible or Talmud. It is used in the Zohar ("Book of Splendor"), a work written in Spain, in the thirteenth century, by Moses de León.[5] The Zohar stands as the chief (but not sole) literary work of kabbalistic thought;[6] Kabbalah, "that which has been received"[7] or "tradition,"[8] is viewed as the sum of Jewish mysticism.[9]

The *Ein Sof* is the timeless transcendental field; the field of no attributes; the no-thingness brimming with infinite possibilities, creativity, intelligence, and organizing power; the source from which everything springs. Rabbi Arthur Green, a leading

---

4. Cooper, *God Is a Verb*, 69–72. Rabbi David Cooper describes this relationship in beautiful detail. Rabbi Bradley Shavit Artson also explores this relationship poignantly in his book on Process Theology. See Artson, *God of Becoming and Relationship.*

5. Matt, *Zohar Annotated and Explained*, xxiv. Some say the second-century Rabbi Shimon bar Yochai was the author of the Zohar. Others say that Moses de León ascribed the work to Rabbi Shimon bar Yochai in order to lend it greater credibility.

6. Scholem, *On the Kabbalah and Its Symbolism*, 1.

7. Matt, *Essential Kabbalah*, 1.

8. Scholem, *On the Kabbalah and Its Symbolism*, 1.

9. Scholem, *On the Kabbalah and Its Symbolism*, 1.

modern-day kabbalistic authority, calls the *Ein Sof* "the hidden root."[10] Gershom Scholem (1897–1982), the great twentieth-century kabbalistic scholar, used the phrase "hidden God."[11] Professor Daniel Matt, an eminent academic and translator of the Zohar, explains that *"Ein Sof* is the God beyond God."[12]

To begin to understand the *Ein Sof* as no-thingness and as the source of creation, we must understand the concept of the *sefirot*. Rabbi David Cooper (1939–2020), a kabbalistic teacher and early contemporary proponent of Jewish meditation, explains in Torah there are ten statements that use the words *va-yomer Elohim*:

> "And *Elohim* (God) said . . ." These ten statements are considered to be divine emanations out of which the world was created. Each emanation is an archetype, which in combination with other emanations provides the mystical elements necessary to form everything in creation, whether physical, emotional, intellectual, or spiritual. The emanations are referred to as *sefirot* . . .[13]

And Professor Matt uses the idea of a process, quoting the thirteenth-century Spanish kabbalist Azriel of Gerona, to describe the *sefirot*: "The ten *sefirot* constitute the process by which all things come into being and pass away."[14]

I like Rabbi Cooper's term "archetypes," as well as the concept that the *sefirot* constitute a "process" of becoming. The *sefirot* are also referred to as "aspects of God's personality,"[15] "stages"

10. Green, *Seek My Face*, 48. Green also describes the *Ein Sof* as the "endless branches," which we will explore later.

11. Scholem, *Major Trends in Jewish Mysticism*, 207–8.

12. Matt, *God and the Big Bang*, 41.

13. Cooper, *God Is a Verb*, 83, 311n1.

14. Matt, *Essential Kabbalah*, 29, 166–67, citing Azriel of Gerona, "Commentary on the Ten *Sefirot*," in Me'ir ibn Gabbai, *Derekh Emunah*, 2b–c, 3a–d.

15. Matt, *Zohar Annotated and Explained*, xxvi.

or "'holy structure' of the inner life of God,"[16] "attributes,"[17] or "energy centers."[18]

Arrangement and Meanings of the *Sefirot*

The *sefirot* are typically portrayed as a series of ten interrelated circles, arranged in three vertical columns:

The Ten *Sefirot*

16. Green, *Ehyeh*, 46.
17. Scholem, *On the Mystical Shape*, 39.
18. Glick, *Walking the Path*, 4.

The *sefirot* (singular: *sefirah*) are most commonly interpreted in two different ways: as together making up the image of a person, and as representing a tree.[19] Below, we will use the image of the tree, but here, first, we will discuss the *sefirot* as the image of a person (facing away from us). Let us begin by briefly describing their names, positions, and attributes.[20]

- The highest *sefirah* is *Keter*, meaning "crown." Positioned in the center, it is the faint, self-propelled impulse within the *Ein Sof* to move from no-thing (*Ayin*) to some-thing (*Yesh*).

- Proceeding down on the right from *Keter* comes *Chochmah*, or wisdom. *Chochmah* is the first unleashing explosion of a point of pure, infinite light, unable to be grasped, into a seed of existence. "Wisdom comes into being out of *Ayin*."[21]

- How can one begin to grasp infinite wisdom? It must be properly channeled and understood. *Binah*, or understanding, is the *sefirah* to the left of *Chochmah*, into which the light of *Chochmah* flows. "*Chochmah* is described as a point of light that seeks out a grand mirrored place of reflection."[22] This place of reflection is *Binah*, which acquires the name "Who,"[23] introducing the first opportunity for contemplation, discernment, and analysis, which "inevitably arouses

---

19. Scholem, *Major Trends in Jewish Mysticism*, 214.

20. The description of the *sefirot* that follows is short and straightforward, intended solely to demonstrate the interrelatedness and Oneness of the *Ein Sof*, the *sefirot*, and God. To better understand the poetry, beauty, and nuance of the *sefirot*, please see, for example, Matt, *Essential Kabbalah*, 1–11; Green, *Ehyeh*, 39–60; Green, "Introduction," in Matt, *Zohar* 1:xlv–liii; Cooper, *God Is a Verb*, 86–91; and Glick, *Walking the Path*, 17–32. For a deep dive, see Gikatilla, *Gates of Light*; this entire book is dedicated to describing the *sefirot*.

21. Matt, "Online Zohar Course," "Reference: Ayin—No-thingness," 2. Job asked: "Wisdom, where is it found?" (Job 28:12). Wisdom comes into being out of *Ayin* (attributed to Asher ben David, cited in Gottlieb, *Ha-Qabbalah*, 84).

22. Green, "Introduction," in Matt, *Zohar* 1:xlvii.

23. Matt, *Zohar* 1:179, n584, 585, 586.

duality."[24] That duality, as we will explore in chapter 6, then becomes the source of conflict (and evil).

The image of *Chochmah* as father and *Binah* as mother, along with the metaphor of primordial conception, is not far beneath the surface. *Binah* "gives birth" to all seven *sefirot* that follow. Daniel Matt writes, "These three highest *sefirot* (*Keter, Chochmah,* and *Binah*) represent the head of the divine body and are considered more hidden than the off-spring of *Binah*."[25]

The next two sets of three *sefirot* each are arranged to the right, left, and center. Consistent with the arrangement of *Chochmah* and *Binah*, on the right they offer a sense of expansiveness and on the left, restraint or discernment. The center *sefirah* represents a place of balance or stability.

- *Chesed*, or lovingkindness, is viewed as the right arm of the divine body. *Din*, or judgment (also referred to as *Gevurah*, or power), is the left arm. The balance of lovingkindness and judgment is the *sefirah* of *Tif'eret*, or beauty, also known as compassion.

- The right leg, *Netzach*, connotes triumph or victory, a sense that anything can be accomplished. The left leg, *Hod*, connotes gratitude, or acceptance for what is.[26] *Yesod*, the *sefirah* in the middle, is referred to as "foundation." It is here that all the attributes from above reassemble and prepare to pass masculine divine energy down to the tenth *sefirah*, *Malchut* (Kingdom), also known as the feminine *Shechinah*.[27]

As we proceed downwards through the *sefirot*, you may be getting a sense of the movement of attributes from subtle to pronounced. The final *sefirah*, the *Shechinah*, more manifest than

---

24. Green, "Introduction," in Matt, *Zohar* 1:xlvii.

25. Matt, *Zohar Annotated and Explained*, xxvi.

26. Kaplan, *Jewish Meditation: A Practical Guide*, 34. Kaplan describes *Netzach* as "dominance" and *Hod* as "submissiveness," although these attributes are not explicitly stated in the Zohar.

27. Green, "Introduction," in Matt, *Zohar* 1:li.

the *sefirot* above, contains all the attributes of those higher *sefirot*, gives birth to the lower worlds, and represents the presence of the divine on earth.

To explain the *Ein Sof*, God, and the *sefirot*, we have had to make distinctions. Is the *Ein Sof* really separate from God? Does God have a head, arms, and legs? Are there ten gods (or Gods), each with different qualities? No, no, and no.

Speaking to these questions, Rabbi Arthur Green teaches that "[*Ein Sof*], God as endless, limitless, undifferentiated reality, is the beginning and the end of truth . . . The ten *sefirot* ('numbers' or stages) within the cosmic structure are not *added* to [*Ein Sof*], but are revealed as existing within it . . ."[28] Elsewhere, Rabbi Green explains it this way:

> One God, but perceived and known in two ways: [YHVH] who transcends and surrounds the world and [YHVH] who fills the world. The transcendent God is entirely faceless. This God is none other than [*Ein Sof*]— that which is without limit, without end, without definition: God as mystery. The God who fills the world has a thousand, a million, a billion infinite faces . . . These two are one, the same God known to us in stasis and in movement, in formlessness and in all forms that exist.[29]

The way the great kabbalistic scholar Gershom Scholem expounds it is this:

> The divine life is expressed in ten steps or levels, which both conceal and reveal [God]. It flows out and animates Creation; but at the same time it remains deep inside. The secret rhythm of its movement and pulse beat is the law of motion of all Creation. As the divine life reveals itself—that is, becomes manifest through its actions on the various levels of divine emanation—it assumes a different shape on each level or, speaking theologically, appears in different attributes. In its totality the individual

28. Green, *Ehyeh*, 39 (emphasis in original).
29. Green, *Seek My Face*, 47.

elements of the life process of God are unfolded yet constitute a unity (the unity of God revealing [God's self]).[30]

Professor Matt, meanwhile, takes us to the Zohar for a closer
understanding:

> the *sefirot* and *Ein Sof* form a unity, "like a flame joined
> to a burning coal." "It is they, and they are it." "They are
> its name, and it is they." From our limited perspective,
> the *sefirot* appear to possess a multiple and independent
> existence. Ultimately, however, all of them are one; the
> true reality is the Infinite.[31]

The gods described here are not different gods; they are the
One God, infused with the One essence, their different attributes
singing the song of life together in perfect harmony.

Above, we used the image of a person to discuss the *sefirot*,
but they can also be discussed using the image of a tree. Here is
how this tree is depicted. Notice it is upside down; its roots are
nourished from the highest level:

30. Scholem, *On the Mystical Shape*, 39.

31. Matt, *Zohar Annotated and Explained*, xxvii–xxviii, citing Sefer Yetzirah 1:7 and Zohar 3:70a, 11b.

The Ten *Sefirot* Depicted as a Tree

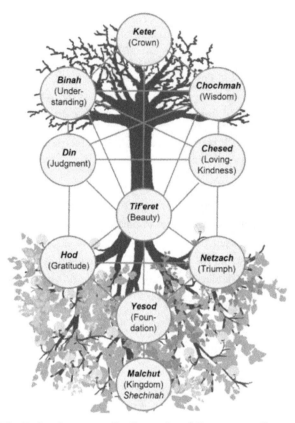

The Bahir (meaning "brilliance" or "illumination") is considered to be one of the earliest Kabbalistic texts and is attributed to the twelfth-century teacher Rabbi Nehunia ben HaKana: "I am the One who planted this tree in order that all the world should delight in it. And in it, I spread All. I called it All because all depend on it, all emanate from it, and all need it."[32] In his translation and commentary on the Bahir, Rabbi Aryeh Kaplan (1934–1983), a twentieth-century scholar of meditation and Kabbalah, clarifies that the tree "refers to the entire array of [s]*efirot*."[33] Scholem further explains:

32. Kaplan, *Bahir*, 9.
33. Kaplan, *Bahir*, 101.

The ten [*sefirot*] constitute the mystical Tree of God or tree of divine power each representing a branch whose common root is unknown and unknowable. But [*Ein Sof*] is not only the hidden Root of all Roots, it is also the sap of the tree; every branch representing an attribute, exists not by itself but by virtue of [*Ein Sof*], the hidden God. And this tree of God is also, is it were, the skeleton of the universe; it grows throughout the whole of creation and spreads its branches through all its ramifications. All mundane and created things exist only because something of the power of the [*sefirot*] lives and acts in them.[34]

So the *Ein Sof* is like the sap of a tree, and the tree is the manifest universe of diversity. The sap flows invisibly, without attribute, throughout the entire tree, and nourishes it; it becomes seen (manifest) as the tree's branches, leaves, flowers, fruit, etc., in all their varied glory. Before the branch manifested as a branch, it was sap . . . and the branch's essence is still sap. Before the leaf appeared as a leaf, it was sap, and its essence is still sap. The same goes for the flower. Same thing with the fruit. And just as the sap of the tree is the essence of all components of the tree, so the *Ein Sof* is the essential makeup of all things in the universe.

• • •

I'd like to digress here for a moment to tie in another well-known teaching, but I want to present a lesser-known perspective on that teaching. When people talk about kabbalistic stories of creation, they often recall the teachings of Rabbi Isaac Luria (1534–1572), the Ari (the Lion), a prominent mystic in the Galilee region of Safed, at that time part of the Ottoman Empire, now Israel. His interpretations are commonly referred to as Lurianic Kabbalah. The Ari teaches, among other things, that when God created the world, God contracted God's infinitely large self in order to "make room" for the world to exist. The eminent twentieth-century Israeli Talmudist and scholar Rabbi Adin Steinsaltz (1937–2020), on the

---

34. Scholem, *Major Trends in Jewish Mysticism*, 214–15.

other hand, teaches the concept of contraction in a different way. Rabbi Steinsaltz writes: "Creation is an emanation from the divine light; its secret is not the coming into existence of something new but the transmutation of the divine reality into something defined and limited—into a world. This transmutation involves a process, or a mystery, of contraction."[35] In other words, the *infinite* infinity of the divine light, the *Ein Sof,* in this analogy "sap," transmutes and contracts itself into the *finite* infinity of the leaf. (These terms, *infinite* infinity and *finite* infinity, are mine.) The leaf (or the fruit or the branch) manifests as *Yesh* (finite some-thing-ness), yet retains *Ayin* (infinite no-thingness) as its essence.

•   •   •

Now, let us relate the four names of God (in addition to *Ein Sof*) that I introduced at the beginning of this chapter directly to the *sefirot.* When we use the name of God "*YHVH,*" we are acknowledging that quality of God's emanation that is the expansive flow of *Chochmah,* wisdom. When we use the name of God "*Elohim,*" we are acknowledging that quality of God's emanation that is *Din,* judgment. When we use the name of God "*Shechinah,*" we are acknowledging the coming together of all God's attributes through the sense of God's embracing presence here on earth.

And what about "*Ehyeh Asher Ehyeh*"? "I Shall Be As I Shall Be" sounds mysterious, as if the God of the future remained unknown to us—perhaps even unknown to God's self as well. I suggested earlier that this name conveys the notion of a dynamic God, a God with whom we have an ongoing, interdependent relationship. What if the line between "we" and "God" were blurred? What are the implications of Scholem's statement that the *Ein Sof* manifests through the *sefirot* as the divine emanations of God revealing God's self? We will explore this further in chapter 6.

35. Steinsaltz, *Thirteen Petalled Rose,* 37.

Everything Is a Manifestation of the Transcendent

I want to delve more deeply here into Rabbi Green's statement that the *Ein Sof* is the endless, undifferentiated source of everything in the world, the hidden God, and that, manifesting through the *sefirot*, it is also "the God who fills the world[, who] has a thousand, a million, a billion infinite faces."[36] When I touch the transcendent, then, I am not only experiencing my own essence; I am also experiencing yours. They are not two different essences that happen to be the same, they are the One Essence.

The *mitzvah* to "love your neighbor as yourself" (Lev 19:18)[37] is also the same teaching. Torah does not say, "Love your neighbor as you love yourself," because then you and your neighbor could be different, even if loved the same. But recognize that at the deepest level, you and your neighbor are the One Self.

Rabbi Dr. Jay Michaelson, a spiritual teacher and political commentator, deeply explores the oneness of creation in his book *Everything is God: The Radical Path of Nondual Judaism*. Rabbi Michaelson writes: "The [Hasidic] movement's founder, Rabbi Israel Baal Shem Tov, and his disciples clearly believed that God filled every corner of the universe and that everything that seems to appear as a separate entity is actually a ripple on the ocean of the Divine."[38]

Deuteronomy 4:35 tells us, "It has been clearly demonstrated to you that YHVH alone is God; there is none else." Rabbi Michaelson explains that historically, this verse has been understood to mean that there is one God, not multiple gods. But from the perspective of nonduality, this verse is interpreted as saying that there is nothing at all beside God.[39] In other words, everything we see manifested in the world, in its essence, is God.

36. Green, *Seek My Face*, 47.

37. Friedman, *Commentary on the Torah*, 382; the Sefaria translation reads "Love your fellow [Israelite] as yourself."

38. Michaelson, *Everything Is God*, 43.

39. Michaelson, *Everything Is God*, 50.

In his book on *Tanya, the Masterpiece of Hasidic Wisdom*, Rabbi Rami Shapiro, a spiritually progressive interpreter of Jewish texts, teaches the same message in slightly different words: "human beings have the capacity . . . to reveal the fact that all beings are manifestations of the One Being, God, or [*Ein Sof*], the Unbounded Infinite. The goal . . . is to awaken to the knowledge of God as all reality, and the realization that you are never separate from or even other than God."[40]

This point has been made again and again, by teachers and scholars all over the world. The contemporary meditation teacher Rabbi Jeff Roth quotes the eighteenth-century Ukrainian Rabbi Menachem Nahum of Chernobyl (1730–1787) as saying:

> What is the world? The world is God, wrapped in robes of God so as to appear to be material. And who are we? We are God wrapped in robes of God and our task is to unwrap the robes and thus dis-cover that we and all the world are God.[41]

The way Rabbi Green puts it is that "God is present throughout Creation. The world is not an entity separate from God, but a cloak that both hides and reveals God's presence."[42]

Finally, let me add the voices of the Hasidic masters who teach that the Hebrew phrase *ein od milvado*, (from Deut 4:35), commonly translated as "there is no other god besides [God]," also means "there is nothing besides [God]—literally. Only [God] exists."[43]

With this perspective in mind, we can reread some familiar texts from the Bible, which we will immediately be able to see in a new light. They are all saying not only "There is one God"; they are in fact saying, "There is nothing, no thing, in the world other than God." God's "exterior" appears different to us in different contexts, as we take it in through our various senses, but the essence of it all

40. Shapiro, *Tanya, the Masterpiece of Hasidic Wisdom*, xxx.

41. Rabbi Menachem Nahum of Chernobyl, cited in Waskow, *Or Chadash*, quoted in Roth, *Me, Myself and God*, 34.

42. Green, *Ehyeh*, 32.

43. Marcus, "Where Is G-d," lines 10, 14. Adapted from the teaching of Rabbi Shmuel of Lubavitch.

is the same. God is all there is. Here are some of these biblical texts; my comments follow each quotation.

Isaiah 6:3: "Holy, holy, holy! The LORD of Hosts! [God's] presence fills all the earth." Or, in a translation many of us are more familiar with: "Holy, holy, holy is the LORD of hosts; the whole earth is full of [God's] glory."[44]

> *Notice that it is God who fills the earth. There is no room for anything other than God. The myriad expressions of creation are nothing more than different attributes or aspects of God,[45] dressed in their unique and varying garb. What is underneath the dressing that appears as creation is nothing but God.*

Isaiah 45:6: "So that they may know from east to west, that there is none but Me. I am the LORD and there is none else."

> *We look around us from left to right and see "different" things, but we are reminded that all those things are manifestations of God.*

Deuteronomy 4:35: "It has been clearly demonstrated to you that YHVH alone is God; there is none else."

> *As we noted above: there is nothing other than God. Everything you perceive is some form or aspect of God.*

Deuteronomy 4:39: "Know therefore this day and keep in mind that YHVH alone is God in heaven above and on earth below; there is no other."

> *You may think that there is something other than God on the earth, but you are mistaken! All this is God. God has just clothed God's self in different garments.*

Psalms 139:7–12: "Where can I escape from Your spirit? Where can I flee from Your presence? If I ascend

44. Jewish Publication Society of America, *"Holy Scriptures,"* 485.

45. I thank Professor Evan Finkelstein for introducing me to the term "aspect of God."

to heaven, You are there; if I descend to Sheol, You are there too. If I take wing with the dawn to come to rest on the western horizon, even there Your hand will be guiding me, Your right hand will be holding me fast. If I say, 'Surely darkness will conceal me, night will provide me with cover,' darkness is not dark for You; night is as light as day; darkness and light are the same."

> *"Darkness and light are the same"—this is a simple, stark way of saying that unity underlies all of diversity. Because the Ein Sof is infinite, it is everything, including all opposites. Infinity gives rise to darkness as well as light, east as well as west, day as well as night. To function in this world, we rely on those differences. Yet, beneath the differences, all is the same . . . it is nothing but God's infinite nature.*

Even the *Shema*, the watchword of our faith, "Hear, O Israel: The LORD Our God, the LORD is one" (Deut 6:4)[46], proclaims this same message: there is one God, and there is nothing that is not God. Rabbi Cooper explains this further, providing a mystical interpretation of the *Shema*: "Listen carefully at the core of your being, the part of you that yearns to go straight to the Source of Life, the transcendent unknowable God and all that we see in the material world surrounding us are, in fact, one and the same."[47]

Transcending—Experiencing the Hidden God

Recapping, then, our texts tell us that:

- the *Ein Sof* is the essence of all of us and of everything in creation;
- we have habituated ourselves to focus on our different, external attributes—after all, we can't function in the world if we do not do so;

---

46. Jewish Publication Society of America, "*Holy Scriptures*," 221.
47. Cooper, *Handbook of Jewish Meditation Practices*, 63.

- and yet, universally, we yearn to enliven the awareness of, and connection with, our essence. That essence that is the "real me"[48] is also the "real you." It is our shared existence, at the deepest level.

It is the "*Ayin*," the no-thingness, the transcendent, that we yearn to experience. As Daniel Matt explains it:

> The essence of serving God and all the [*mitzvot*] is to attain the state of humility . . . You attain this humility through the awe of God's vastness, through realizing that "there is no place empty of it." Then you come to the state of [*Ayin*], the state of humility. You have no independent self and are contained in the Creator. This is the meaning of the verse: "Moses hid his face, for he was in awe." Through his experience of awe, Moses attained the hiding of his face, that is, he perceived no independent self. Everything was part of divinity.[49]

This experience that we yearn for, the experience of losing our individual, independent self and simply being one with divinity, is a very direct and immediate experience. It does not require a fancy conceptual apparatus. Rabbi Roth teaches:

> In order to free ourselves from the constraints of conceptual thinking, we have proposed a mystic path that emphasizes direct experience. Instead of *conceptualizing* the Divine Presence, analyzing it, or talking about it, we rather strive to *experience* it moment by moment in our lives.[50]

Furthermore, this direct and immediate experience that we yearn for, that we so desire, is not just something that we *want*; it is something we *need*. In his book *Man's Quest for God*, Rabbi Abraham Joshua Heschel (1907–1972), using the word "prayer" to talk about how we connect with God, tells us that our desire for that

48. Kaplan, *Jewish Meditation: A Practical Guide*, 87.

49. Matt, *Essential Kabbalah*, 72, 184, quoting from Issachar Baer of Zlotshov, *Mevasser Tsedeq* (Berditchev, 1817), 9a-b; see Schatz-Uffenheimer, *Ha-Hasidut ke-Mistiqah*, 114.

50. Roth, *Me, Myself and God*, 85 (italics in the original).

connection is "an *ontological necessity*, an act that constitutes the very essence of man. He who has never prayed is not fully human. Ontology, not psychology or sociology, explains prayer."[51] What Heschel is saying is that connecting with, awakening, enlivening, and exploring our own deepest being and existence is how we grow to become more ourselves. He explicitly states that the purpose of prayer is to take us beyond emotion to the field of transcendence: "prayer goes beyond the scope of emotion; it is the approach of the human to the transcendent."[52]

Prayer, in other words, takes our awareness beyond emotion. Elsewhere, Heschel uses the word "piety" to teach that our goal is to take our awareness not only beyond emotion, but beyond intellect as well:

> Although piety implies a certain spiritual profundity, it is not an outgrowth of innate intelligence. Its forces spring from purity of heart rather than from acumen of mind . . . It is the regard for the transcendent, the devotion to God, that constitute its essence . . . Piety is the realization and verification of the transcendent in human life.[53]

Rabbi Roth, addressing this same concept—the concept of devotion to God, to the divine—uses the more common word "prayer" and talks about its goal: "Prayer is the process of aligning our attention to the Divine Presence."[54]

Rabbi Green, finally, in his book *Radical Judaism*, describes his own experience of transcending: "I . . . consider the sacred to be the most important and meaningful dimension of human life. 'The sacred' refers to an inward, mysterious sense of awesome presence, a reality deeper than the kind we ordinarily experience."[55] And again, elsewhere: "I am sometimes able to enter into states of inner

51. Heschel, *Man's Quest for God*, 78 (italics in the original). Heschel references *Netivot Olam*, a text written by the Talmudic scholar, mystic, and philosopher Rabbi Jehuda Loew ben Bezalel (Maharal) of Prague (ca. 1525–1609).

52. Heschel, *Man's Quest for God*, 13.

53. Heschel, *Moral Grandeur*, 309–10.

54. Roth, *Jewish Meditation Practices*, 70.

55. Green, *Radical Judaism*, 4.

openness to a nameless and transcendent presence, that which I choose to call 'God.'"[56]

Our teachers and our texts remind us time and time again that our goal is to *directly experience* God's great transcendental silence—not just to discuss it, feel it, or think about it. It is the nature of our being—our own essential nature—and we are never not connected to it. In chapter 4, I will recount some of the practices the sages used in past centuries to enliven their connections with the transcendent.

Devekut—Cleaving to God

Once we have had that experience of our own true, silent essence, what is the next step? Our texts tell us that the next step is to cling to it. (The Hebrew word is *devekut,* meaning to "cleave," to "hold fast.") We want to have that awareness of God's infinite presence at all times. In fact, it is demanded of us; it is one of our *mitzvot:* "You must revere YHVH: only your God shall you worship, to [God] shall you hold fast, and by God's name shall you swear" (Deut 10:20).

Using this verse, Rabbi Kaplan also talked about this cleaving to God, this attachment. Citing Rabbi Josef Caro (1488–1575), one of the prominent kabbalists (and traditionalists—as the author of the Shulchan Aruch) of the sixteenth century in Safed, Rabbi Kaplan wrote:

> This is the mystery of Unity, through which a person literally unifies [one's self] with [one's] Creator. The soul attaches itself to [God], and becomes one with [God], so that the body literally becomes a dwelling place of the Divine Presence. This is what the Torah means when it says, "You shall fear God your Lord, and you shall serve [God] and attach yourself to [God]."[57]

56. Green, *Radical Judaism*, 1.

57. Kaplan, *Meditation and Kabbalah*, 178 (Maggid Mesharim, BaShalach 15 Shevat, p. 56c).

Rabbi Kaplan explains that possessing a "holy spirit," *Ruach HaKodesh*, is often used to describe enlightenment.[58] King David prays for continuous enlightenment using these words: "Do not cast me out of Your presence, or take Your holy spirit (*Ruach Ha-Kodesh*) away from me" (Pss 51:13). From this verse we may conclude that cleaving to God, or the continuous awareness of God's holy spirit, is what constitutes enlightenment.

Following are a few more passages from our biblical texts that reinforce and expand our understanding of this *mitzvah* of cleaving to God, expressing it in a variety of ways, using different language:

> Psalms 16:8: "I am ever mindful of the LORD's presence; [God] is at my right hand; I shall never be shaken."

> Deuteronomy 30:19–20: "Choose life—if you and your offspring would live—by loving your God YHVH, heeding God's commands, and holding fast to God."

> Deuteronomy 26:17: "You have affirmed this day that YHVH is your God, in whose ways you will walk, whose laws and commandments and rules you will observe, and whom you will obey."

> Psalms 105:4: "Turn to the LORD, to [God's] might; seek [God's] presence constantly."

> Proverbs 3:6: "In all your ways acknowledge [God], and [God] will make your paths smooth."

> Song of Songs 5:2: "I was asleep, but my heart was wakeful. Hark, my beloved knocks!"

Rabbi Green describes this *devekut,* this cleaving to God, with these words:

> In its highest form it may indeed be described as mystical union, a moment when the self is completely absorbed and overwhelmed by the reality of oneness, the climax of religious experience. Yet it also allows for the soul to return to itself, enriched and even transformed by the

58. Kaplan, *Meditation and the Bible*, 17.

unitive moment but still able to live and act as a separate spirit—indeed, still able to maintain its existence within the body.[59]

This description of *devekut* is important because it puts the goal of cleaving to God within our grasp. We can experience a sense of union with God and, *at the same time*, go about our own day-to-day lives.

Rabbi Kaplan writes about the ability to do both of these things simultaneously—to go about daily life while also maintaining our union with God—with reference to the eighteenth-century mystic, healer, rabbi, and kabbalistic practitioner from Poland known as the "Baal Shem Tov," or "Besht":

> It is significant to note that the Baal Shem Tov (1698–1760), founder of the Hasidic movement, made use of this [the 119th] Psalm. He was taught by his spiritual Master that if he said the 119th Psalm every day, he would be able to speak to people, while at the same time maintaining a transcendental state of attachment to the Divine.[60]

Maimonides used the metaphor of romantic love to talk about attachment to God. Maimonides's metaphor of the lover is conveyed by Rabbi Elie Kaplan Spitz, a twenty-first-century scholar of Jewish spirituality and Jewish law, this way:

> What is the love of God that is befitting? It is to love the Eternal with a great and exceeding love, so strong that one's soul shall be knit up with the love of God, and one should be continually enraptured by it, like a lovesick individual, whose mind is at no time free from his passion for a particular woman, the thought of her filling his heart at all times, when sitting down or rising up, when he is eating or drinking.[61]

59. Green, *Radical Judaism*, 70.

60. Kaplan, *Meditation and the Bible*, 142, referencing *Shivechey HaBaal Shem Tov*, 98 (*Shivechey HaBaal Shem Tov* is a collection of legends about the Baal Shem Tov).

61. Spitz, *Does the Soul Survive?*, 27, referencing *Mishnah Torah* Book One, Knowledge: "Laws of Repentance," 10:6, using the translation of Twersky, *Maimonides Reader*, 84.

Rabbi Michaelson quotes Rabbi Aharon of Staroselye (in present-day Belarus) (1766–1828), who described the difference between how we usually experience the world and experiencing it in unity with God as seeing from "our point of view" and from "God's point of view," respectively. Michaelson continues, "Both points of view are of the same reality—they are just different points of view. Ours sees objects, people, and things. God's sees only Godself. The object is to see both as two sides of the same coin."[62]

We will discuss this concept further in chapter 3, within the discussion of Adam and Eve.

The *Ein Sof*, Its Manifestation, and Modern Physics

Sages and philosophers argue over what the true reality is. Some proclaim that if it is the unmanifest that is the *true* reality, then the hammer on my workbench is simply an illusion. But last weekend, when that hammer hit my finger instead of the nail (as I am not the first student of philosophy to notice!), it didn't seem like an illusion to me. There are different levels of truth; they all maintain their own integrity concurrently.

That hammer hurt my finger when it hit it, but at the sub-atomic level, the composition of the hammer's head and of the air around it don't appear to be significantly different. At the sub-atomic level, there is not much there, either in the hammer or in the molecules comprising the air, aside from lots of space between the few electrons whizzing around the nuclei of atoms, at great distances from each other.

There is a growing body of literature on the nexus of modern physics and religion. While we have described the manifestation of the world here by proceeding from the no-thingness of the *Ein Sof* through the quality-inducing *sefirot*, physicists work backwards, from objects, through molecules and atoms, to subatomic particles in order to try to understand the most basic scientific makeup of the universe. They simplify as they get deeper, literally looking for

---

62. Michaelson, *Everything Is God*, 8.

a unified field from which everything springs. Unified Field Theory was developed in the late twentieth century, theorizing that the four known forces could all be described mathematically as having a common set of properties. The four forces are:

- electromagnetism—the force that acts on electrically charged particles;

- weak force—the force that accounts for radioactive decay and a star's energy;

- strong force—the force that holds subatomic particles together to form the nucleus of the atom; and

- gravity—the force that causes particles to attract.

Electricity and magnetism had been thought to be separate forces until 1864, when the Scottish mathematician and scientist James Clerk Maxwell demonstrated that they were one.[63]

Modern physics has shown that electromagnetism and the weak force, although superficially appearing quite different (the weak force is 10 million times weaker than the electromagnetic force), are "different facets of a single, more-fundamental electroweak force."[64]

The next step currently being pursued is called "grand unification." That theory proposes that the electroweak force and the strong force share the same underlying properties and can be united.[65]

Proof of a "unified field," "an attempt to describe all fundamental forces and the relationships between elementary particles in terms of a single framework" has not yet been accomplished.[66] At the heart of this research is the Higgs boson, a particle discovered in 2012 and confirmed in 2013. Equations point to the Higgs boson as the one particle that gives mass to all particles through

---

63. Stewart, "James Clerk Maxwell," para. 7.

64. Sutton, "Electroweak Theory," para. 1.

65. Sutton, "Unified Field Theory," para. 5.

66. Sutton, "Unified Field Theory," para. 1.

its interaction with them. For this reason, it is often referred to as the "God particle."[67]

This book, however, is not about science but about religion. My point is simply that science and religion may follow different paths as they explore and attempt to understand our universe. In addition, science and religion will use different language to describe that universe. But the different paths they take, and the different words they use, need not deny or negate one another. Instead, they may inform each other as we humans continue the search for the deepest truths in our lives.

67. Sutton, "Higgs Boson," paras. 1, 3.

Chapter 3

Connecting with God throughout Jewish History

WE HAVE BEEN EXAMINING the building blocks of the nature of creation as well as the nature of God's self. The mystical and the traditional texts use different language, but their messages are consistent and complementary. God is One. God is the creator. God created/creates everything out of nothing. Everything in the world is a manifestation of God's infinite nature. There is no thing in the world other than God. We yearn to connect with God, our essence. (Or, rather: We yearn to become more aware of our *already existing* connection with God, our essence, and to enliven that connection.) And we want to be aware of that connection at all times. Let us examine some of the ways in which we have connected with God throughout our history.

Adam and Eve

Let us begin at the beginning and look at a portion of the story of Adam and Eve:

> And from the ground God YHVH caused to grow every tree that was pleasing to the sight and good for food, with the tree of life in the middle of the garden, and the tree of knowledge of good and bad . . . And God YHVH commanded the Human, saying, "Of every tree of the garden you are free to eat; but as for the tree of knowledge of good and bad [some translations read: "evil"], you must not eat of it; for as soon as you eat of it, you shall die." (Gen 2:9, 16, 17)

What was happening in the "days" leading up to this scene? God was creating the universe. How? By bringing forth diversity/duality out of unity. On the first day, God separated the light from the darkness (Gen 1:4–5). On the second day, God created a firmament to separate the upper waters from the lower waters (Gen 1:6–8). On the third day, God separated the waters beneath the firmament from the dry land, creating earth and seas (Gen 1:9–10). On the fourth day, God separated the day from the night (Gen 1:14).

So why does the construction of our world rely on separation, on duality? Because that is the inherent nature of our physical existence. If everything were the same, there would be nothing to distinguish. We would have, in effect, only what we had before the universe was created: oneness, no differences.

And yet, after creation, that is still exactly what we have: nothing but the Ein Sof, "spread out far and wide." Everything just looks (and sounds, tastes, smells, and feels) different on the outside. God manifests God's hidden Self through the attributes of the ten *sefirot*.

Recall our depiction of the *sefirot* in chapter 2 as an upside-down tree. What about the tree is real? Is the sap real? Yes, it is the source that feeds everything else. Are the fruit, leaves, and branches real? Yes, you can be nourished by them, enjoy their shade, and build furniture from them.

Both the hidden and the manifest values of the *Ein Sof* are real, but they appear to us, concurrently, as different levels of reality. I alluded to this in chapter 2 when I talked about the hammer, the air, and my thumb. When the hammer hits my thumb, it sure feels real. But at the quantum level, there are no more physical subatomic particles in the head of the hammer than there are in the air around it. Both realities—first, that the hammer is solid, and second, that the hammer is a few particles whizzing around a lot of nothing—are true at the same time, but at different levels of existence.

What does this have to do with Adam and Eve and the trees (now switching to a different metaphor about trees) in the Garden of Eden? In the Garden of Eden, all life was lived in complete harmony because differences and attributes were not yet prominent in the awareness of the inhabitants (i.e., they did not know they were naked) (Gen 3:7). As God was creating the world, the Garden of Eden represents a symbolic transition from unity to diversity. To use our previous tree metaphor: the *Ein Sof*, the quality of God's wholeness (the sap), still dominated Adam's and Eve's awareness.

God warned Adam and Eve not to transfer their attention away from the wholeness of existence by focusing on differences—which is what would happen if they ate from the tree of knowledge of good and evil (the knowledge of differences). Once they had eaten from the tree of knowledge of differences, the fruit (and branches and leaves) would dominate their view of reality, and they would lose sight of the sap, the *Ein Sof*. They would see the world, its contents, and its inhabitants as separate and unrelated entities. They would become mortal. This "death" would occur because they had permitted the eternal, never-dying nature of the *Ein Sof* to recede into the background of their awareness. They would have let themselves be identified primarily as the ever-changing, living and dying, leaves, flowers, and fruit of the tree—rather than the sap.

Here, from the Zohar, is a slightly different perspective, though it still reinforces the mandate to perceive from a place of unity: "But this tree is a tree of death; whoever takes it alone dies, for he has taken deadly poison."[1] What does it mean to "take it alone"? Daniel Matt explains that the tree represents *Shechinah* (the lowest of the *sefirot*, God's immanent presence on earth), and that "anyone who partakes of Her alone separates Her from the other *sefirot*, thereby cutting off the vivifying flow of emanation,

1. Matt, *Zohar* 1:222.

37

which is replaced by a deadly poison."[2] After eating from the tree, Adam and Eve were not able to maintain the entirety and intrinsic oneness of *all* the *sefirot* (all the attributes of God) in their awareness.

The fate of Adam and Eve is similar to that of Elisha ben Avuya (Aher, the other), who entered paradise with Ben Azzai, Ben Zoma, and Rabbi Akiva, as described in Talmud (b. Ḥag. 14b). At a critical time, Aher, too, failed to perceive from a place of oneness; he "severed the saplings," meaning he lost sight of the wholeness of the *sefirot*, and died.[3]

Returning to Adam and Eve: of course, they had to eat that fruit. Otherwise there would be no need for Torah, or for life as we know it. Torah is the guidebook for our multidimensional life here in earth. If we were living a life of complete oneness and harmony in the Garden of Eden, we wouldn't need a guidebook. Torah reminds us that we, along with everything around us, are eternal, and that we share the same essence. Torah gives us instructions on how to act in order to bring out the qualities of interconnectedness in our lives, which only appear to be comprised of separate beings and entities.

In chapter 2, we briefly discussed Rabbi Aharon of Staroselye, quoted by Rabbi Michaelson as describing the difference between seeing from "our point of view" and from "God's point of view."[4] Torah asks us to see from God's point of view. Both points of view are looking at, and taking in, the same reality—they just see it from different perspectives. Ours sees objects, people, and things. God's sees only God's self. Can we learn to appreciate both in the same glance?

Why did God set it up this way—making God's wholeness our essential makeup, but then designing a universe that intrinsically forces us to live in differences, only so that we can then reconnect with our oneness and be guided by that oneness in everything we do? Rabbi Shneur Zalman of Liadi (1745–1812), the

2. Matt, *Zohar* 1:222n936.

3. Matt, *Zohar* 1:222–23n937.

4. Michaelson, *Everything Is God*, 8.

founder of Chabad Hasidism, frames the purpose of creation more succinctly: "The purpose of the creation of the worlds from *Ayin* [no-thingness] to *Yesh* [some-thing] was that they be transformed from *Yesh* to *Ayin*."[5]

Why is it set up this way? I don't know. Perhaps it's set up this way so that we can all enjoy the variety of God's bounty while here on earth, in a way that uplifts us all together as one. All we know is that Torah tells us that *this is our job*: to enliven the connection with the oneness, the godliness within us; to know it in everything else; and to act accordingly.

Four Levels of Connection

How do we "find our way back" to our source? (I put the phrase "find our way back" in quotes because in fact we are never not connected to our source—just like a leaf is never not connected to its essence, the sap.) There are an infinite number of paths back. Since the *Ein Sof* is the essence of everything, and everything is a manifestation of the *Ein Sof*, then anything is potentially a pathway back to our oneness. We can find our way back through anything we do; anything we hear, touch, see, taste, or smell; anything we feel; or anything we think. A mountain vista carries some people back—for others it is the embrace of a child, a prayer, a song, a kind deed, or even a memory.

Let us explore how the Kabbalists taught this concept. The prophet Ezekiel describes the Lord coming upon him through the vision of four mystical creatures (seen from lowest to highest): a wheel-like creature, an angelic being, a throne, and a "man" upon the throne.[6] This vision is often referred to as Ezekiel's chariot (*merkava*). The Kabbalists explain that Ezekiel was seeing the four supernal universes, which are said to have the following associations with the four creatures:

---

5. Matt, "Online Zohar Course"; "Reference: Ayin—No-thingness," 4.
6. Kaplan, *Meditation and the Bible*, 35–36, describing Ezekiel, ch. 1.

- The wheel-like creature is a "form," which signifies the Universe of Making, called *Assiyah*.

- The angelic being signifies "angels," which is the Universe of Formation, called *Yetzirah*.

- The throne signifies the Universe of Creation, called *Beriyah*.

- And the man on the throne signifies the divine emanations, the ten *sefirot*, which is the Universe of Closeness, called *Atzilut*.[7]

These universes are alluded to in the Bible (Isa 43:7) when God proclaims that God will redeem "All that is called by My name, for My Glory (*Atzilut*), I have created it (*Beriyah*), I have formed it (*Yetzirah*), and I have made it [*Assiyah*]."[8] These verses tell us that we are able to connect with God at many levels:

- *Assiyah* (Hebrew for "made") is manifested as doing;

- *Yetzirah* (Hebrew for "formed") is manifested as feeling;

- *Beriyah* (Hebrew for "created") is manifested as thinking; and

- *Atzilut* (Hebrew for "my glory") is manifested as being.[9]

From doing, to feeling, to thinking, to being. Notice the evolution. It moves from obvious to subtle; it develops from physical to emotional to mental and then beyond, to simply being.

These ascending levels of connection are deeply rooted in Judaism in other ways as well. Our rabbis teach that our souls have levels that correspond to these universes:

- *Assiyah* corresponds to the soul level *nefesh*, the wisdom of the body;

- *Yetzirah* corresponds to the soul level *ruach*, the wisdom of the emotions;

7. Kaplan, *Meditation and the Bible*, 35–37.
8. Roth, *Me, Myself and God*, 40; Kaplan, *Meditation and the Bible*, 36. Kaplan's translation.
9. Roth, *Me, Myself and God*, 40; Kaplan, *Meditation and the Bible*, 35–37.

- *Beriyah* corresponds to the soul level *neshama*, the wisdom of thought; and

- *Atzilut* corresponds to the soul level *chaya*, the wisdom of being or mystery.[10]

And when we study and interpret Torah, we do that at four corresponding levels as well, the names of which, taken together, make up an acronym that becomes the Hebrew word **PaRDeS** (meaning "garden" or "orchard"):

- *Pshat*—the plain or literal meaning;

- *Remez*—the allegorical connection, a hint or an allusion that we sense;

- *Drash*—the homiletical or interpretive lesson that we understand; and

- *Sod*—the mystical secrets it contains.[11]

But what are we to make of all these parallels? The message is that God connects with us at many levels. Let's explore these levels by associating a few of the *mitzvot* with each of them. Note: All of the *mitzvot* can be understood at all levels.[12] However, some present themselves to me most forcefully at certain levels.

At the *Assiyah*, or straightforward physical, level, the nexus of connection is there when you are helping your neighbor (whom you might not even like that much) push their stalled car out of the street into their driveway. This is performing the *mitzvah*: "When

10. Roth, *Me, Myself and God*, 40; Roth, *Jewish Meditation Practices*, 147–50; Kaplan, *Meditation and the Bible*, 35–37; Michaelson, *Everything Is God*, 30–31. The rabbis also teach about the fifth level, *Yechidah*. See also Shapiro, *Tanya, the Masterpiece of Hasidic Wisdom*, xxxvi–xli. Rabbi Schneur Zalman of Liadi (the "Alter Rebbe"), the founder of Chabad Hasidism and author of Tanya (Chabad Hasidism's treatise on Jewish spirituality), teaches that the ultimate level of the soul, *Yechidah*, unity or oneness, is another level beyond *Chaya*. For simplicity, as do some others, I group *Chaya* and *Yechidah* together.

11. My Jewish Learning, "Approaches." Note, however, that Daniel Matt (*Zohar Annotated and Explained*, 2) and Gershom Scholem (*Major Trends in Jewish Mysticism*, 210) teach the order as PDRS.

12. I am grateful to my friend Mat Kozinetz for reminding me of this.

you see the ass of your enemy lying under its burden and would refrain from raising it, you must nevertheless help raise it" (Exod 23:5).

At the *Yetzirah*, or emotional, level, the feeling of connection may arise when you give to the poor, performing the *mitzvah*: "You shall not pick your vineyard bare, or gather the fallen fruit of your vineyard; you shall leave them for the poor and the stranger: I YHVH am your God" (Lev 19:10).

At the *Beriyah*, or intellectual, level, the understanding of connection may arise when calculating compensation for a robbery: "that person shall repay the principal amount and add a fifth part to it" (Lev 5:23–24).

All of the above are channels, pathways through which to experience connections with God.

But what about the channel of *Atzilut*, the connection that takes us directly to God's transcendental nature, the mystical level of pure being or, as Rabbi Kaplan describes it, "pure consciousness?"[13] Can we expand our repertoire of connection pathways to include that one as well? Furthermore, can we make that connection occur regularly and reliably?

Our kabbalistic sages pursued that goal, particularly around the sixteenth century in Safed, largely through meditation practices. We will discuss the history of Jewish meditation briefly in chapter 4. And we will explore the implications of having regular, repeated experiences of the *Ein Sof* in chapter 5.

But some might argue that, for the last two thousand years, using the three lower levels (and even occasionally the fourth), the connection to God has been achieved well enough, regularly enough, reliably enough, and deeply enough for our parents, their parents, and their parents' parents. Why, then, some will ask, aren't these levels of connection good enough for me and my children? My answer is: they very well may be. You may simply not feel the need to explore the Kabbalists' approach to connecting directly with the *Atzilut*, the level of being.

13. Kaplan, *Meditation and the Bible*, 2.

However, while we find intellectual and emotional satisfaction and meaning through our practice of the *mitzvot*—even if they do not (or do not regularly) transport us to the depth of our souls—many people, myself included, are also looking to go beyond the emotional and intellectual levels. Through our practices, we want our intellect and emotions to be overtaken by Heschel's sense of a "universal stillness"—of transcendence. When that happens, it is a restorative experience we never forget.

Many will argue that if we are not connecting with God at the depth that we wish, then we are not following the *mitzvot* closely enough. If only, this argument goes, we prayed regularly three times a day, wore *tzitzit*—the ritual fringes that we are commanded to wear to remember and observe the *mitzvot* (Num 15:37–41), observed Shabbat, ate a kosher diet, put on *tefillin*—two small boxes with prayers inside that are wrapped on the forehead and arm during weekday morning prayers (Deut 6:5–8), gave to the poor, and so on . . . *that* would bring us closer to God. Following the *mitzvot* more closely in traditional ways in order to connect more deeply with God is a time-honored approach that you may want to adopt, or may have already adopted, either in addition to or instead of meditative practices. The traditional, familiar Jewish texts are deep and wide in their teachings of how to connect with God through the levels of *Assiyah, Yetzirah,* and *Beriyah.* And the various ways in which we connect with God are not mutually exclusive. They are additive. In my case, for instance, I have begun to observe the laws of kosher eating more closely (though not yet fully), and since 2014 I have been wearing *tzitzit.* The practice of saying the prayer while putting on *tzitzit* in the morning slows me down for just a moment and reminds me to maintain awareness of my deeper responsibilities throughout the day. To date, it has not provided me an experience of transcendence.

Our mystical texts, however, which have been less frequently studied over the last five hundred years, communicate more clearly that we can connect with God directly at the level of *Atzilut.* This inward approach may be, for many, more easily attainable, and the connection that it allows us more sublime. We will explore these texts in greater depth in chapter 4.

The Connection—A Changing Dynamic

It would be an endless task to discuss all the ways in which we have connected with God throughout history and to cite examples from our texts. It could be argued that Jewish texts are nothing but laws, lessons, and stories about connecting with God and with each other. Therefore, I will focus here on just a few instances of connection, often referring to well-known stories. I have chosen examples to illustrate not only that our ancestors connected with God through many pathways, but that their connections had many different qualities.

Sometimes the connection was simply a sense of God's presence, felt through silence, verse, love, music, dreams, and other experiences. Sometimes the connection involved listening to and responding to God, a response that was often to follow God's instructions, but sometimes the opposite: not to follow but rather to argue and negotiate with God, or simply disobey God.

The instances on which I draw will highlight that when we connect with God, the dynamic between us and God is ever changing. Our understanding of our relationship with God has not been a linear progression, but roughly speaking, in the early days, God was portrayed as the micromanaging boss, controlling all the outcomes (after all, God did unilaterally create the world). Later, God would listen to us complain or argue, and might or might not decide to make a change based upon what we had to say. After the laws (Torah) were given, God delegated their interpretation to us—especially as we prepared to enter the Promised Land. We will even read one well-known story in which God tries to interpret a question of law, and the rabbis actively decline to listen.

How should we describe this ever-changing God/human dynamic and our own evolving understanding of it? I suggest that we can view it from the mystical perspective of nonduality. The line between God and us blurs. To quote Menachem Nahum of Chernobyl once again: "What is the world? The world is God, wrapped in robes of God so as to appear to be material. And who are we? We are God wrapped in robes of God and our task is to unwrap the robes and thus dis-cover that we and all the world are God."[14] When things happen in the world, who acts to make them happen? We will explore this God/human dynamic more fully below and in chapter 6, when we discuss the coming (hopefully sooner rather than later!) of the Messianic Age.

Feeling God's Presence

Silence

One could argue that the simplest form of connecting with God may be through silence. This is worth pointing out, given that speaking and listening, the counterpoints to silence, play an out-sized role in the traditions of the Jewish people. In the beginning, "God *said*, 'Let there be light'; and there was light" (Gen 1:3, my emphasis). And all Jews proclaim, "*Hear*, O Israel: The LORD our God, the LORD is one."[15] (Deut 6:4, my emphasis).

When Aaron's sons were killed for offering alien fire to God, Aaron connected with God in silence. The story began like this:

> Now Aaron's sons, Nadab and Abihu, each took his fire pan, put fire in it, and laid incense on it; and they offered before YHVH alien fire, which had not been enjoined upon them. And fire came forth from YHVH and consumed them; thus they died at the instance of YHVH. (Lev 10:1–2)

How did Aaron react to this tragedy? "And Aaron was silent" (Lev 10:3). Aaron found solace and consolation by easing back into wholeness. At the level of emotion and intellect, there was too much dissonance for Aaron to absorb. In the infinite vastness of the ocean, however, our frenetic drops of water find refuge.

14. Rabbi Menachem Nahum of Chernobyl, cited in Waskow, *Or Chadash*, quoted in Roth, *Me, Myself and God*, 34.

15. Jewish Publication Society of America, "*Holy Scriptures*," 221.

Then, in this well-known verse (1 Kgs 19:11–12) God is speaking to Elijah, who hears God's voice in silence:

> And [God] said, "Go forth and stand upon the mount before the LORD." And, behold, the LORD passed by, and a great and strong wind rent the mountains, and broke in pieces the rocks before the LORD; but the LORD was not in the wind; and after the wind an earthquake; but the LORD was not in the earthquake; after the earthquake a fire; but the LORD was not in the fire; and after the fire a still, small voice.[16]

We hear a similar message in Mishnah (`Abot 3:13, the ethics of our ancestors), "A fence to wisdom is silence."

The book of Psalms also reiterates that we can hear God in silence: "Truly my soul waits quietly for God; my deliverance comes from [God]" (Pss 62:2).

Today, silence continues to be an important vehicle for connection. In all Jewish denominations, silent prayer is an important component of our *Siddur*, our prayer book.

Verse

King David connected with God through verse, among other things. In the Psalms, David praised God, thanked God, and asked God for protection. Notice that many of the Psalms begin "A psalm of David" (Pss 23:1, for example). Others (for example Pss 24:1) begin "Of David. A psalm."

Talmud (b. Pesaḥ. 117a) teaches us, "If a psalm begins: Of David a psalm, this teaches that the Divine Presence rested upon him first and afterward he recited the song. However, if a psalm opens with: A psalm of David, this teaches that he first recited the song, and afterward the Divine Presence rested upon him."[17]

16. Jewish Publication Society, "*Holy Scriptures*," 433. Or in a different, beautiful translation: Matt, *Becoming Elijah*, 28, "a sound of sheer stillness."

17. See also Kaplan, *Meditation and the Bible*, 167–68n71.

Music

The prophet Elisha used music to help him quiet his intellect and become attuned to God. When seeking a prophetic message, he said "now then, get me a musician." And then, "As the musician played, the hand of the LORD came upon him" (2 Kgs 3:15).[18]

The Psalmist sings, "Then I will acclaim You to the music of the lyre for Your faithfulness, O my God; I will sing a hymn to You with a harp, O Holy One of Israel. My lips shall be jubilant, as I sing a hymn to You, my whole being, which You have redeemed" (Pss 71:22–23).

Love

The Song of Songs, or *Shir ha-Shirim*, is an entire poetic book of the Bible dedicated to conversations between two lovers as they pursue each other "through vineyards and fields of blossoming flowers. It is traditionally understood as a metaphor for the loving relationship between God and the people of Israel."[19] Rabbi Green teaches a *midrash* (interpretation) that the famous second-century sage Akiva said, "Had the Torah not been given, the world could have been conducted by the Song of Songs alone."[20]

I have experienced this teaching firsthand. Coming out of meditation, I have felt a deep sense—or really energy—of love. I use the term "energy" because what I specifically experienced was that energy was propelling the universe forward. The words that came to me—hackneyed, I know—were "Love makes the world go 'round." Now I understand how we can have a deep spiritual experience and then spontaneously connect that experience with an idea or belief we have adopted in our lives.

18. See Kaplan, *Meditation and the Bible*, 63.

19. "Living Library of Jewish Texts."

20. Green, *Judaism for the World*, 91, referencing Schechter, *Agadat Shir Hashirim*, line 22; see also Schechter's notes there.

Transcendental Judaism

Dreams

As we will see in the next section, God has spoken to many of our prophets through dreams, often sending them messages or instructions to follow. In the case of Jacob, described below, Jacob becomes aware of God's presence in a dream during which God reiterates the covenant between God and the children of Abraham.

We pick up the story here: Esau is furious with his brother Jacob, not only for having forced Esau to trade his birthright to Jacob in exchange for a bowl of lentils, but also for tricking their father, Isaac, into giving a blessing meant for Esau (as the older son and Isaac's favorite) to Jacob instead. Following his mother's advice to leave for a while until Esau has calmed down, Jacob sets off to find a wife from among his relatives in the region of Paddan-Aram. On the way,

> [Jacob] had a dream; a stairway was set on the ground and its top reached to the sky, and messengers of God were going up and down on it. And standing beside him was YHVH, who said, "I am YHVH, the God of your father Abraham's [house] and the God of Isaac's [house]: the ground on which you are lying I will assign to you and your offspring." (Gen 28:12–13)

Because the *Ein Sof* is hidden within the subtlest level of everything, everywhere, including ourselves, we can find God wherever we are. Jacob realizes this. "Jacob awoke from his sleep and said, 'Surely YHVH is present in this place, and I did not know it.' Shaken, he said, 'How awesome is this place! This is none other than the abode of God, and that is the gateway to heaven'" (Gen 28:16–17).

In his book *God Was in This Place & I, i Did Not Know*, Rabbi Lawrence Kushner, a prolific author on Jewish spirituality and mysticism, provides us with seven interpretations of Jacob's statement, each at a different level of meaning. These range from simple awareness ("If I had known God was here, I wouldn't have gone to sleep")[21] through self-reflection ("God was here because I stopped

21. Kushner, *God Was in This Place*, 21.

being aware of myself")[22] all the way to "The Self of the Universe" ("I is the Lord your God").[23]

From this mystical perspective, Kushner offers a magnificent *midrash* in which Jacob, after realizing that one of God's names may be "I," is speaking with Moses de León, the author of the Zohar.

> Jacob says, "Suppose one of God's Names is: 'I, *Anochi* [the Hebrew letters: *aleph, nun, kaf, yud*]'. Now the verse reads 'Surely God was in this place, but by the Name, 'I, *Anochi* [*aleph, nun, kaf, yud*], i did not know.'"[24]

To clarify, the lowercase "i" above is Jacob referring to himself as initially not knowing that "I" was one of God's names.

> "Oh, God!" whispered Jacob. "That means that God and I both call ourselves by the same name. And (the logic was simple) if God's Name is I (*Anochi*—[*aleph, nun, kaf, yud*]), then God must also have a Self". . . "this is the name each self has for its self. And since the gesture of self-reference—the way by which I evoke who I am—is the same for every self, whenever we say 'I' we evoke not only the 'I' of every other soul, we echo the primary 'I,' '*Anochi*, [*aleph, nun, kaf*]' of Sinai . . . We are made of the same holy stuff. It has this mysterious ability to look different in each pair of eyes, to sound different in each voice, but it is all the same."[25]

We may look outside ourselves for God, but if we do so, we have forgotten that God's essence *is* our essence; God has never been apart from us. Jacob's epiphany—"Surely the Lord is present in this place, and I did not know it"—is realizing that the Lord is present with him in every place he goes.

Rabbi Aryeh Kaplan offers a similar insight when he relates the "I" of God to the "I" of the individual self. Kaplan uses the less formal Hebrew word for "I," namely "*ani.*"

---

22. Kushner, *God Was in This Place*, 83.

23. Kushner, *God Was in This Place*, 129.

24. Kushner, *God Was in This Place*, 132.

25. Kushner, *God Was in This Place*, 133.

What is the real me? A hint to the answer can be found in the Hebrew word for "I," *ani* [*aleph, nun, yod*]. It is significant to note that if the letters of *ani* are rearranged, they spell the word *ayn* or [*Ayin*] (*aleph, yod, nun*), which denotes nothingness. This would seem to imply that the real "me" is the nothingness within me.[26]

The Children of Israel

The ability to feel God's presence is not limited to our patriarchs or prophets. All of the children of Israel feel God's presence, and respond to God, in a variety of ways.

In Egypt, all of the children of Israel witnessed the ten plagues that God inflicted upon the Egyptians, but it was Moses and Aaron who interacted directly with God.

As the Israelites fled Pharoah, they witnessed the presence of God as cloud or fire, depending on whether it was day or night:

> YHVH went before them in a pillar of cloud by day, to guide them along the way, and in a pillar of fire by night, to give them light, that they might travel day and night. The pillar of cloud by day and the pillar of fire by night did not depart from before the people. (Exod 13:21–22)

Soon after that, the Israelites were trapped between the Egyptian army and the sea. "Greatly frightened, the Israelites cried out to YHVH. And they said to Moses, 'Was it for want of graves in Egypt that you brought us to die in the wilderness?'" (Exod 14:10–11). Torah doesn't tell us what, exactly, the Israelites may have said to God. But it seems the conversation they wanted to have was not with God, but with Moses.

Even at Sinai, after receiving the Ten Commandments, our ancestors needed an intermediary between themselves and God:

> All the people witnessed the thunder and lightning, the blare of the horn and the mountain smoking; and when the people saw it, they fell back and stood at a distance.

26. Kaplan, *Jewish Meditation: A Practical Guide*, 87.

"You speak to us," they said to Moses, "and we will obey;
but let not God speak to us, lest we die." (Exod 20:15–16)

And that was the time-honored model for communication:
God spoke to Moses and Moses spoke to the people, or the people
spoke to Moses and then Moses spoke to God (for example Exod
17:2–5). It is not uncommon for us to read, "YHVH spoke to
Moses, saying: 'Speak to the Israelites and say to them . . . '" (for
example Num 6:1–2).

After a couple of years in the desert, the Tabernacle was set
up. Through the absence or presence of a cloud, God signaled to
the Israelites whether and when they should move or stop, but
God's communications still went primarily through Moses:

> Whether it was two days or a month or a year—however
> long the cloud lingered over the Tabernacle—the Israel-
> ites remained encamped and did not set out; only when
> it lifted did they break camp. On a sign from YHVH they
> made camp and on a sign from YHVH they broke camp;
> they observed YHVH's mandate at YHVH's bidding
> through Moses. (Num 9:22–23)

Finally, there was a breakthrough (even if temporary): the
people spoke directly to God. After Aaron died and had been
mourned, the Israelites continued their journey. They were approaching the land of Canaan, the Promised Land, when the Ca-
naanite king

> engaged Israel in battle and took some of them captive.
> Then Israel made a vow to YHVH and said, "If You deliv-
> er this people into our hand, we will proscribe [destroy]
> their towns." YHVH heeded Israel's plea and delivered
> up the Canaanites; and they and their cities were pro-
> scribed. (Num 21:1–3)

Finally, as the Israelites were leaving the wilderness and entering the Promised Land, their relationship with God was transformed once again. For forty years, their every need had been met
by God, even though they did not always appreciate it at the time!
The sea parted, food fell from heaven, water gushed from rocks,

enemies were repelled, their itinerary was provided. But entering the Promised Land, the Israelites would have to learn how to deal with the practical side of life on their own.

Responding to God

Noah

"YHVH saw how great was human wickedness on earth—how every plan devised by the human mind was nothing but evil all the time" (Gen 6:5). "YHVH said, 'I will blot out from the earth humankind whom I created—humans together with beasts, creeping things, and birds of the sky; for I regret that I made them.' But Noah found favor with YHVH . . . Noah was a righteous man; he was blameless in his age [generation]; Noah walked with God" (Gen 6:7–9).

When God told Noah to build the ark, he did it—exactly according to God's specifications. And, on God's instruction, Noah collected male and female of all that lived so that the earth could be repopulated after the flood. "Then YHVH said to Noah, 'Go into the ark, with all your household'" (Genesis 7:1), and Noah did so.

Noah followed God's instructions to the letter. Yet Noah is not looked upon favorably by the sages. Why not? Noah only looked out for himself and his family. He did not speak out against the evil actions of others in his time (though in his defense, the sages also say that no one would have listened). When Torah says that Noah was "blameless in his age," is that a compliment or a criticism? Was Noah such a great guy, or was he only good in comparison to the low bar that was in place at that time?

The faith leader, moral philosopher, and author Rabbi Jonathan Sacks (1948–2020) teaches that

> [The Hasidim] called Noah a *tzaddik im peltz*, "a righteous man in a fur coat." There are essentially two ways of keeping warm on a cold night. You can wear a thick coat, or you can light a fire. Wear a coat and you warm

only yourself. Light a fire and you can warm others too. We are supposed to light a fire.[27]

Thus, although Noah connected with God and did God's bidding, his legacy is tainted.

Abraham

Many of us are familiar with God's command in Genesis to Abram commonly translated as: "Go forth from your native land and from your father's house to the land that I will show you" (Gen 12:1).

We understand that God is telling Abram to strike out towards something new. To leave behind what he knows and to trust that God will guide him on his path forward.

Several modern commentators remind us that the Hebrew here uses the reflexive of the verb "to go," which translates as: "Go to yourself,"[28] "Get going to yourself,"[29] or, "Go to yourself, to know yourself, to refine yourself."[30]

And what is the outcome of being able to connect to that self, that essence in Abram (and all of us) that is the "hidden God"? In exchange for doing so, God promises Abram:

> I will make of you a great nation, and I will bless you; I will make your name great, and you shall be a blessing. I will bless those who bless you and curse the one who curses you; and all the families of the earth shall bless themselves by you. (Gen 12:2–3)

In other words, Abram will be able to follow God's lead more clearly and will be supported by God. Abram will become a great nation, he will be blessed, and his name will be great. Not only will Abram benefit directly, but others whose lives are touched by his will be affected as well: they will reap rewards if they are aligned with Abram, and they will incur curses if they are not.

27. Sacks, "Righteousness Is Not Leadership," para. 23.
28. Glick, *Living the Life of Jewish Meditation*, 61.
29. Roth, *Me, Myself and God*, 58.
30. Matt, *Zohar* 2:9n62.

Of course, this call is not just a call to Abram. According to the Polish Hasidic teacher Rabbi Yehudah Aryeh Leib Alter, the Sefat Emet (1847–1905), this call to self-realization is a message spoken to every one of us.[31]

Let us look at another story about Abraham. In this story, Abraham is negotiating with God about God's plan to destroy the city of Sodom, due to the sins of its inhabitants. "[W]ill You then wipe out the place and not forgive it for the sake of the innocent fifty who are in it?" Abraham asks God. When God agrees not to do that, Abraham presses God further . . . what if there are forty-five innocents, or forty, thirty, twenty, or, finally, ten? God agrees that destruction will not be meted out to everyone, in deference to even ten among them who are innocent (Gen 18:24–32).

In biblical times, God unilaterally controlled events on earth according to God's will. And so it was in this case as well. But here, for the first time, we begin to get a foreshadowing that humans, or at least Abraham, might be able to have at least some influence over what God does here on earth.

The Prophets

God said, "Hear these My words: When prophets of YHVH arise among you, I make Myself known to them in a vision, I speak with them in a dream" (Num 12:6). For many prophets, this experience is described simply through words: In Jeremiah (Jer 1:2), "The word of the LORD came to him." Isaiah declares (Isa 1:2), "For the LORD has spoken." Obadiah proclaims (Obad 1:1), "We have received tidings from the LORD." Ezekiel had the vision of the chariot, which we have already discussed. The book of Malachi opens more dramatically (Mal 1:1), "A pronouncement: The word of the LORD to Israel through Malachi."

The prophets receive their messages from God, messages that typically involve instructions to chastise the people for acting wickedly and to threaten them with various forms of punishment

---

31. Frankel, *Wisdom of Not Knowing*, 17, citing Alter, *Sefat Emet*, 79.

unless they repent and change their ways. The prophets then go out among the people and deliver the message, often at great personal risk to themselves.

But not all prophets "get it" the first time. When the word of the Lord came to Jonah, he immediately fled in the opposite direction, found himself on a ship in a storm, was swallowed by a giant fish where he lived for three days, and was finally spewed out onto dry land. At that point, "Jonah went at once to Nineveh in accordance with the LORD's command" (Jonah 1:1—2:11, 3:3).

Moses

In contrast to the other prophets, Moses is the prophet to whom God speaks "mouth to mouth, plainly and not in riddles" (Num 12:8). Moses has many interactions with God, running the gamut from obedience (e.g., following God's instructions on how to deal with Pharoah, Exod 7:14–20) through complaint (e.g., being exasperated with the Israelites' grumbling over conditions in the desert, Exod 17:4), argument (e.g., talking God out of destroying God's "stiffnecked" Israelites who created the Golden Calf, Exod 32:9–14), and negotiation (see the discussion below), to disobedience (e.g., hitting the rock twice to get water from it rather than speaking to it, Num 20:11).

Let's explore the classic example of Moses negotiating with God, which occurs at Moses's first meeting with God. Moses is tending the flock of his father-in-law, Jethro, when

> A messenger of YHVH appeared to him in a blazing fire out of a bush. He gazed, and there was a bush all aflame, yet the bush was not consumed. Moses said, "I must turn aside to look at this marvelous sight; why doesn't the bush burn up?" When YHVH saw that he had turned aside to look, God called to him out of the bush: "Moses! Moses!" He answered, "Here I am." (Exod 3:2–4)

We all know what happens next. God tells Moses that God has heard the plight of God's people, and God will rescue them.

The only catch is that God is going to send Moses to Pharaoh to announce the plan. Moses declines, saying he can't do it; it's too much for him. God shows Moses a couple of miracles to convince him that God has the power necessary to pull this off. They continue to argue back and forth. Finally, angry with Moses, God decides to send Aaron along to help (Exod 3:5—4:31).

As part of this conversation,

> Moses said to God, "When I come to the Israelites and say to them, 'The God of your fathers' [house] has sent me to you,' and they ask me, 'What is [God's] name?' what shall I say to them?" And God said to Moses, "*Ehyeh-Asher-Ehyeh*" [I Shall Be As I Shall Be]." (Exodus 3:13–14)

How can we interpret this name, "I Shall Be As I Shall Be"? This is one case where we might actually be within our rights to envision this God as bearded and male, the old man sitting on a throne up in heaven causing plagues to occur, seas to part, and manna to fall from the skies. After all, those events are exactly the ones that are going to happen next. Reflecting this moniker "I Shall Be As I Shall Be," God, as the old bearded man, plays His hand close to the vest; God keeps us guessing. Nobody tells God what to do or how to be. God metes out justice exactly as God sees it. From our perspective, God may treat nations or individuals more harshly than we think God should (thus we call God "vengeful"). Or, alternatively, we may believe that God treats them more charitably than we think God should (thus earning from us the adjective "compassionate"). In any case, viewing God in this manner, God is the actor separate from us, God will be whatever God wants to be, and we are the objects of God's actions.

As we discussed above, in the context of Abraham negotiating with God about the future of Sodom—God will listen to us and consider our requests. Moses, of course, also negotiates with God, successfully influencing the outcome, beginning with this meeting at the burning bush.

Negotiating the Calendar and Holy Days

God makes a high-level pronouncement about when the month of Passover is to start, but delegates the detailed decision-making to God's people. Torah tells us, "This month shall mark for you the beginning of the months" (Exod 12:2; regarding the time for the Pesach sacrifice, see Exod 12:6). The renowned American scholar and teacher Rabbi Irving (Yitz) Greenberg reminds us that it is the rabbinic court, not God, that determines when a month begins. Because the lunar phase cycle (from new moon to new moon) takes 29.5 days, the length of each month (whether 29 days or 30) requires human calculation and judgment. Rabbi Greenberg reminds us that "Judaism is a covenant-partnership in which the human partner plays a central—even authoritative—role."[32] The great American Talmudic scholar Rabbi Joseph Soloveitchik (1903–1993) taught that

> God said: Before Israel became My people, the festivals were "the festivals of the Lord." But henceforth the festivals are those "which ye shall proclaim"... The Holy One, blessed be He, has, as it were, stripped Himself of His ornaments—i.e., His dominion—and has handed it over to Israel, to the earthly court. The earthly court decrees, and the Holy One, blessed be He, complies.[33]

Pesach Sheni (Second Chance Passover)

Here, God sets the exact day of the month and time of day for the festival to begin, only to change that ruling after being confronted by the people who explain to God the complications of day-to-day living.

Here is the beginning of the story:

32. Greenberg, "Hebrew Calendar," "GreenbergParashatBo5781," 3. Rabbi Greenberg goes on to cite Soloveitchik below. I am grateful to Rabbi Debbie Stiel for bringing this source to my attention.

33. Soloveitchik, *Halakhic Man*, 81, referencing Deuteronomy Rabbah (a homiletic commentary on the book of Deuteronomy) 2:14.

> YHVH spoke to Moses in the wilderness of Sinai, on the first new moon of the second year following the exodus from the land of Egypt, saying: Let the Israelite people offer the passover sacrifice at its set time: you shall offer it on the fourteenth day of this month, at twilight, at its set time; you shall offer it in accordance with all its rules and rites. (Num 9:1–3)

But scarcely three verses later, an objection is raised:

> But there were some householders who were impure by reason of a corpse and could not offer the passover sacrifice on that day. Appearing that same day before Moses and Aaron, those householders said to them, "Impure though we are by reason of a corpse, why must we be debarred from presenting YHVH's offering at its set time with the rest of the Israelites?" Moses said to them, "Stand by, and let me hear what instructions YHVH gives about you." (Num 9:6–8)

And the Lord immediately responds, saying that these men may offer the sacrifice one month later (Num 9:11).

In other words, a law is set forth by God, but circumstances that are brought to God's attention by the people cause God to amend the law.

Esther

The book of Esther is unique in that it is the only book in the Hebrew Bible that does not contain the name of God; God's face is hidden here (*hester panim*, "I will keep My countenance hidden"—Deut 31:18). And yet, even in God's absence, the people manage to save themselves from annihilation. The heroine of this story is Queen Esther (whose name sounds a lot like the *hester* of *hester panim*). Mordecai tells her, "if you keep silent in this crisis, relief and deliverance will come to the Jews from another quarter, while you and your father's house will perish. And who knows, perhaps you have attained to royal position for just such a crisis" (Esth 4:14). Esther then immediately leaps into action, not waiting for intervention from "another quarter" (in other words, God): she declares a fast for herself and the Jews of Shushan, in order to prepare her to successfully confront the king and convince him to destroy Haman and save the Jews. As the Torah scholar Rabbi David Kasher teaches,

> It is up to the heroes of the story—Mordechai, and particularly Esther—to save the day. Esther, counsels Mordechai, must reveal her Jewishness to her husband the King, in order to secure his protection for her people. Which she does, at great personal risk—and successfully. The Jews are saved, thanks to the great bravery of Esther. God, it seems, is not the savior in this story.[34]

The Oven of Akhnai

In this well-known story from Talmud (b. B. Meṣ. 59b), God attempts to intervene and make rulings, but is barred from doing so. In the story, Rabbi Eliezer is attempting to prove his point about the ritual purity of an oven. To defend his argument, he calls upon a carob tree to change its location, a stream to flow backwards, and walls to crumble—all of which they do. He even calls on heaven to support him. God attempts to support him, but Rabbi Yehoshua reminds God of God's words in Deut 30:12 that "It [the Torah/ the law] is not in heaven." Rabbi Yirmeya adds, "Since the Torah was already given at Sinai, we do not regard a Divine Voice, as You already wrote at Mount Sinai in the Torah: 'After a majority to incline' (Exod 23:2)." In other words, God wrote that it is the *people* who shall now interpret Torah and define outcomes, not God. And later we learn what God's response to that was: "The Holy One, Blessed be He, smiled and said: 'My children have triumphed over Me, My children have triumphed over Me.'"

---

34. Kasher, "Hidden Face," para. 23.

The Daughters of Zelophehad

After the incident of Baal-peor, when Pinchas slew the idolators and God stopped the plague, God called for a census by tribe of the Israelite men able to bear arms. God decreed that the land should be apportioned based upon that census (Num 26:1–2).

> The daughters of Zelophehad . . . Mahlah, Noah, Hoglah, Milcah, and Tirzah . . . stood before Moses, Eleazar the priest, the chieftans, and the whole assembly, at the entrance of the Tent of Meeting, and they said, "Our father died in the wilderness. He was not one of the faction, Korah's faction, which banded together against YHVH, but died for his own sin; and he has left no sons. Let not our father's name be lost to his clan just because he had no son! Give us a holding among our father's kinsmen." Moses brought their case before YHVH. And YHVH said to Moses, "The plea of Zelophehad's daughters is just: you should give them a hereditary holding among their father's kinsmen; transfer their father's share to them." (Numbers 27:1–7)

Sarah Yehudit Schneider, a Torah teacher and the founder of the correspondence school A Still Small Voice, references midrash, an interpretation of the law (Yalkut Shimoni, Pinchas 27), that imagines the conversation between a skeptical Moses and the daughters, who, through the clarity and purity of their arguments, convince Moses of the justice of their complaint. Moses then "immediately presented their case before [God]." Moses became their advocate, not only because of the intellectual strength of their petition, but because the daughters felt the injustice at a deep, spiritual level and were looking for the truth; this was not an ego issue for them.[35]

Schneider draws out the meaning, for Jews through the ages and today, of the story about Zelophehad's daughters, as well as the midrashic commentary on that story:

---

35. Schneider, "Daughter," lines 35–145.

Though the written Torah is fixed and final, the Oral Torah is constantly evolving. Each generation has new tech-
nologies and cultural phenomena with halachic [Jewish
legal] implications that have not yet been explored. The
process of formulating questions and generating halachic discourse is the lifeblood of the Jewish people. The
daughters of [Zelophehad] are role models for this labor
of applying Sinaitic law to contemporary situations.
Every Jew in every generation has a part to play in this
process of the evolution of the Oral Tradition.[36]

Or, as the Torah commentary scholar Rabbi Kasher, whom I
quoted earlier, writes about this situation:

[Some] say, what can we do? Our hands are tied. A law
is a law if the Torah says it is. We can express our compassion, but we cannot undo what God has done. Apparently, however, God can—and does—undo what God
has done. But God does not do so unilaterally. God waits
for us to make the case. God is waiting for us to be wise.
God is waiting for us to seek justice. God is waiting for
the righteous to come forth and receive their reward.[37]

• • •

In the examples given above, God has final control over the outcomes, but is willing to be persuaded by Abraham, by Moses, and
by Mahlah, Noah, Hoglah, Milcah, and Tirzah. God is absent while
Esther saves the day. And in the story of the Oven of Akhnai, God
attempts to participate, but is reminded by God's children that
God has already delegated decision-making to them. The God/
human dynamic is not static.

What is our modern view of God? Few of us today still envision God as a bearded man on a throne in heaven. But many of us
do hold a belief that God is a separate entity, apart from us, who
plays some role in determining outcomes in the world. And this
is not an unreasonable belief. After all, for the last 3,500 years we

36. Schneider, "Daughter," lines 88–94.
37. Kasher, "Women of Valor," paras. 48–50.

have been praying to God, offering praise and thanks, and asking for assistance, forgiveness, and comfort.

In chapter 6, we will push the envelope of this dynamic and explore it from a different perspective, the perspective of nonduality.

Chapter 4

An Overview of Jewish Meditation

IN GENESIS, CHAPTER 24, Abraham is now an old man, and his son, Isaac, is not yet married. Abraham sends his servant Eliezer on a mission to find a wife for Isaac, "not . . . from the daughters of the Canaanites among whom I dwell, but . . . [from] the land of my birth" (Gen 24:1–4). Eliezer has successfully completed the mission and is on his way back from Nahor with Rebekah (Isaac's soon-to-be wife) and her nurse. "And Isaac went out walking in the field toward evening and, looking up, he saw camels approaching" (Gen 24:63). Sefaria, Inc. translates the Hebrew word *suach* (*sin vav chet*) as "walking," then footnotes it as "meditating." Rabbi Aryeh Kaplan tells us that this word means "to meditate" and occurs only this one time in the Bible. *Suach* is related to *siyach* and *sichah*, which are also translated as "meditate" and occur abundantly in Psalm 119[1]; this is the Psalm that the Baal Shem Tov would recite daily to enable him to "speak to people, while at the same time maintaining a transcendental state of attachment to the Divine,"[2] as we saw in chapter 2.

1. Kaplan, *Meditation and the Bible*, 101, 165n1.

2. Kaplan, *Meditation and the Bible*, 142, referencing *Shivechey HaBaal Shem Tov*, 98.

Other words meaning "meditation" are derived from the root *hagah* (*hey, gimmel, hey*), and occur a few times throughout the Bible.[3] The best-known may be the phrase "Let the words of my mouth and the meditation (*hagayon*) of my heart, be acceptable before Thee, O Lord, my Rock, and my Redeemer"[4] (Pss 19:15).

Finally, there are other words that imply meditation either because they evoke sublime experiences (for example, words like "glow," "delight," "rejoicing") or because they frequently appear near such words.[5] Thus, there is a variety of linguistic evidence of meditation in the Bible.

What I want to do now is explore the ways in which our sages practiced meditation. But first, let us remind ourselves of the goal of meditation. Why do we meditate? Why did and why do our sages meditate? It is a sublime way to achieve, enhance, or enliven a connection with God; a way to experience oneness. Or, as Rabbi Steve Fisdel (1948–2019), a Kabbalist, longtime meditation teacher, and founder of the Center for Jewish Mystical Studies in Albany, California, writes: "The true, primary objective of meditative practice within Jewish tradition is *yichud*, unification with God."[6]

Meditation Techniques of the Sages

In this section, I describe some of the meditation techniques that the sages used to let their attention return home, to return to the divine. These descriptions are not instructions. For one thing, as I note below, the secrets to many of these practices are currently lost. And for those seeking specific how-to help, there are, as I describe in the afterword to this book, many resources available that provided detailed meditation instruction, in the form of books, apps, websites, and in-person instruction.

---

3. Kaplan, *Meditation and the Bible*, 111.
4. Jewish Publication Society, *Holy Scriptures*, 788.
5. Kaplan, *Meditation and the Bible*, 119–29.
6. See Fisdel, "Meditation as Our Own Jacob's Ladder," 121.

Unifications (*Yichudim*)

The idea of unifying God's name is as old as Judaism itself. The *Shema*, "Hear, O Israel: The LORD our God, the LORD is one" (Deut 6:4) is recited during morning and evening prayers and before retiring at night.[7] It proclaims the oneness of God and declares, as we described earlier, that there is nothing other than God.

Rabbi Isaac Luria was a developer and proponent of *yichudim*, or unifications, and viewed them as some of the most important meditation techniques for obtaining enlightenment (which we defined in chapter 2 as cleaving to God, or the continuous awareness of God's presence). The primary purpose of unification (*yichud*) meditation is to move our experience of dualism or diversity toward the experience of unity. One unification exercise involves interweaving the letters of different names of God, or the letters related to multiple *sefirot*, in our mind, thus unifying them in our awareness.[8] For example, we can merge the letters of YHVH with ADoNaY, yielding YAHDVNHY, and then repeat that sound in our mind.[9]

Another type of unification (*yichud*) is to bind different names of God together and then imagine moving these unifications up the ladder of the four supernal universes that we discussed in chapter 3. Rabbi Kaplan gives the following example:

> The lower soul (*nefesh*) is from the Universe of [*Assiyah*], which is associated with the name *Adonoy*. One should therefore meditate on the name *Adonoy*, binding it to the name *YHVH* in the Universe of [*Assiyah*]. He should then bind this to the name *Ehyeh* in the Universe of [*Assiyah*]. He should then meditate on this, elevating the name *Ehyeh* of [*Assiyah*], and binding it to *Adonoy* of *Yetzirah*. [One proceeds in this manner through the Universes of *Yetzirah*, *Beriyah*, and *Atzilut*], step by step, until he reaches *Ehyeh* of *Atzilut*. He should then bind

7. "Shema," lines 8–9.

8. Kaplan, *Meditation and Kabbalah*, 218–19 and Verman, *History and Varieties*, 192–93.

9. Verman, *History and Varieties*, 192.

Ehyeh of *Atzilut* to the very highest level, which is the Infinite Being [*Ein Sof*].[10]

Nullification (*Bitul*)

Like unifications, *bitul*, or nullification meditation, is intended to raise and attach one's awareness to the highest level, the awareness of no-thingness, *Ayin*. One way to accomplish this is by nullifying one's ego. As the Hasidic master Rabbi Nachman of Breslov (1772–1810), a great-grandson of the Baal Shem Tov, writes, "One must include himself in God's unity, which is the Imperative Existence. A person cannot be worthy of this however, unless he nullifies his ego, and it is impossible to accomplish this without meditation."[11]

Rabbi Kaplan describes techniques for visualizing no-thingness such as imagining the blackness of empty space or the transparency of empty space without any background color. He teaches that "if one visualizes nothingness and at the same time clears the mind of thought, the mind becomes a total blank. The mind is then at its most sensitive, open to even the most ethereal experiences."[12]

Describing nullification, Rabbi Steve Fisdel, teaches that "this is the level in all universes that is not constricted. When a man nullifies himself completely and attaches his thoughts to Nothingness, then a new sustenance flows to all worlds."[13] We will discuss this concept further in chapter 6, in the section on "Touching the Source."

---

10. Kaplan, *Meditation and Kabbalah*, 225.

11. Kaplan, *Meditation and the Bible*, 15, referencing Rabbi Nachman, *Likutei Moharan* 52. (See Likutei Moharan 52:5 in Sefaria.) Rabbi Nachman refers to meditation as *hitbodedut* here. See discussion of *hitbodedut*. As I describe below, there is overlap to these techniques.

12. Kaplan, *Jewish Meditation*, 85.

13. Fisdel, *Meditation Practice*, 118.

Permutations

As we noted in chapter 2, from ten utterances using the phrase "and God said" (*va-yomer Elohim*), the world was created. One of Judaism's earliest mystical texts is the *Sefer Yetzirah,* meaning "Book of Creation." It is a short, enigmatic poem that tells the tale of the creation of the universe. The *Sefer Yetzirah* teaches that God creates the world through the 22 letters of the Hebrew alphabet, and that the ten *sefirot* provide the dimensions of reality that structure the universe.[14] Thus, the "words" that God spoke (the many permutations and combinations of the 22 letters) comprise the components of the universe.

That is why a meditation technique that involves permuting letters has been regarded as a way to align one's awareness with the infinite creative power of God. As Rabbi Kaplan teaches, "if an individual knows how to correctly manipulate the letters of the alphabet, he is able to make use of the same spiritual forces that originally brought the universe into being."[15]

Rabbi Abraham Abulafia of Zaragoza, Spain (1240–1296), one of the great kabbalistic meditation teachers, was a developer and proponent of permutation meditations. One of Rabbi Abulafia's most fundamental techniques involves chanting and permuting the letters of God's name, YHVH, with the primary vowel sounds *oh, ah, aa, ee,* and *uu.* This meditation also integrates head movements that represent the vowel sounds as they are chanted.[16]

Rabbi Jill Hammer has written a translation and compelling commentary of the *Sefer Yetzirah.* She offers new visualizations and meditations associated with each of its 49 verses to help her

14. Hammer, *Return to the Place,* viii, xvii. I have simplified here the complex process that Rabbi Hammer describes in her introduction. She notes that the qualities of the *sefirot* described in the *Sefer Yetzirah* are different from those introduced in the Zohar (which was published later). In this book, I refer to the qualities of the *sefirot* as described in the Zohar.

15. Kaplan, *Meditation and Kabbalah,* 77.

16. Cooper, *Ecstatic Kabbalah,* 20–22.

readers imagine and internalize the mystical vibrations of creation, thus connecting them with the energies of the cosmos.[17]

Isolation (*Hitbodedut*)

Hitbodedut means self-isolation. Abraham Maimonides (1186–1237), the son of Moses Maimonides, taught that this means isolating oneself both externally and internally. Rabbi Kaplan explains external isolation simply involves being alone physically—often out in nature, anywhere away from other people.[18] But then what does one do once one is alone? Rabbi Cooper explains that speaking aloud to God is an integral part of the practice. One says whatever comes to one's heart and mind, and that might include utterances of praise, thanks, or request. This may feel uncomfortable at first, but it is a way to open the lines of communication in preparation for the next level of experience, ultimately attaining *devekut*.[19]

The next level of *hitbodedut* is the practice of internal self-isolation. The great Kabbalist Rabbi Chaim Vital of Safed (1543–1620) taught that "one must seclude himself (*hitboded*) in his thoughts to the ultimate degree," separating the soul from the body.[20] And Rabbi Levi ben Gershon of France (1288–1344), known as the Ralbag, explained this isolation further, as "the isolation (*hitbodedut*) of the consciousness from the imagination, or both of these from the other perceptive mental faculties."[21]

As with *yichudim* (unification) and *bitul* (nullification) meditations, the goal in isolation, or *hitbodedut*, is to transcend our thoughts and bodily sensations and let our awareness return to what Rabbi Kaplan refers to as "pure consciousness," the *Ein Sof*.

---

17. Hammer, *Return to the Place*.

18. Kaplan, *Meditation and the Bible*, 5.

19. Cooper, *Handbook of Jewish Meditation Practices*, 59–61.

20. Kaplan, *Meditation and Kabbalah*, 15, referencing Vital, *Shaarey Kedushah*, Part Four, 15b.

21. Kaplan, *Meditation and Kabbalah*, 15–16, referencing Rabbi Levi ben Gershon, *Milchemat HaShem*, 19a (2:6).

Rabbi Kaplan describes this as "a normal definition of the meditative state, and it is the end result of all successful meditation."[22]

Concentration

Concentration meditations involve aiming one's attention toward, or focusing one's attention on, a certain thought, object, or meaning.[23] The idea behind this practice is the concept that the things on which we place our attention become more prominent in our lives. If we feel we want to be more compassionate, we focus our attention on that. Or perhaps we are trying to enhance in ourselves courage, flexibility, or equanimity. Generally, our meditation teachers teach us to sit quietly, perhaps begin by focusing on our breath, and then introduce the desired object of our attention. For example, if we want to increase our sense of gratitude, we can focus on the Hebrew phrase "I am thankful"—*modeh ani* for men, *modah ani* for women. Say the words to yourself over and over. Dwell on them. Inhale, feeling your gratitude; exhale, returning your gratitude.[24]

The meditation teacher Dr. Nan Fink Gefen notes that "sometimes meditators experience an 'open space' around the single point on which they are focusing. Here they become deeply connected with God in a state of *devekut*. Or they become one with the Holy, so that the separate self dissolves into a state of non-duality."[25] The phenomenon that Dr. Gefen is describing is the fact that sometimes a concentration meditation can unexpectedly go deeper than the object of focus and morph into a transcendental experience.

---

22. Kaplan, *Meditation and the Bible*, 2.

23. Roth, *Jewish Meditation Practices*, 20–21.

24. See Gefen, *Discovering Jewish Meditation*, 94–97 for a more complete description of this practice.

25. Gefen, *Discovering Jewish Meditation*, 43.

Visualization

Visualization meditations are a form of concentration meditation. In concentration meditation, we give our attention to an idea, or a concept: our awareness becomes immersed in it, and in our awareness it is enhanced. Sometimes visualizing the idea rather than, or in addition to, thinking about it can help us integrate the idea more deeply, transforming and expanding it in our awareness. Rabbi Yoel Glick, a teacher of mysticism and Jewish meditation, describes an example of this: a visualization meditation on the blue thread (*tekhelet*) of the *tzitzit*. Rabbi Glick writes:

> We are told in the Talmud [Ḥul. 89a] that the blue of the *tekhelet* resembles "the color of the sea, and the sea is like the deep sky, which resembles the color of the sapphire stone, which resembles the color of the Throne of Glory." When we look at the *tekhelet*, our mind is lifted through a series of images that stretch our awareness out toward the Infinite.[26]

Contemplation (*Hitbonenut*)

Contemplation meditation is different from concentration meditation. Contemplation meditation, or *hitbonenut*, begins by putting one's complete attention on an object. The object could be a leaf, a stone, one's hand, or even the stars in the sky. The idea is to see and absorb the completeness of the object so fully, so clearly, and so intently that one begins to see *beyond* the surface level to some deeper level of the object. In so doing, we see and understand our deepest selves through our relationship with another aspect of creation. We move towards experiencing the oneness (or interrelatedness) of all things in creation.[27]

A number of years ago I had such an experience, although it came about spontaneously. I was at home in Phoenix, sitting down

26. Glick, *Living the Life of Jewish Meditation*, 70–73.
27. Kaplan, *Jewish Meditation*, 67–69.

to lunch by myself. As I often do while eating alone, I probably had a weekly newsmagazine open to read while I ate. What was on my plate, I have forgotten. But the glass of milk that I picked up became alive. As I was raising the milk to my lips the milk "said" to me, "Here I am. My sole purpose on earth has been for this moment: to nourish you today. It is my joy to fulfill that destiny." At that moment, I felt a calm and a surge of joy and gratitude, and a sense of awe at the organizing power of God: at how the cow, the grass, the dairy farm, the delivery truck, the supermarket, and countless other forces came together to make this happen.

Moses Maimonides taught that *hitbonenut* helps us to achieve a "profound love for God . . . because [*hitbonenut*] is not merely a simple contemplation of various aspects of God's creation, but is understanding oneself as part of this creation."[28] Based on my experience of complete calm, awe, and interconnectedness that I describe above, I can confirm Maimonides' teaching. And King David expressed the same feeling in one of the Psalms: "When I behold Your heavens, the work of Your fingers, the moon and stars that You set in place, what is man that You have been mindful of him, mortal man that You have taken note of him" (Pss 8:4–5).

Intention (*Kavanah*)

Intention is similar to concentration, except that intention is a desire for a goal or outcome (whether general or specific) that is set and then released. You may have heard the expression "Let go and let God." That expression might have its origin in Psalms (Pss 46:11) which reads "Desist! Realize that I am God" (or, a more familiar translation expanded upon by Professor Robert Alter: "Let go, and know that I am God"). Professor Alter writes that the etymology of the Hebrew translated here as "desist" or "let go" involves "relaxing one's grip on something."[29] With intention, we set a direction and then move forward from there. Our intention

28. Kaplan, *Jewish Meditation*, 50–51.
29. Alter, *Hebrew Bible*, 3:123n11.

might be a request to God. It might inform our thoughts or actions throughout the day, week, or month, or it might serve as a beacon for longer-term navigation in our lives.

Music/Chanting/Repetition

In chapter 3, we referenced a few places in the Bible where music was used to feel God's presence. Music alone, without words, gives our intellect a rest, permitting it to quiet down and become attuned to its subtler levels.

Chanting words or phrases can accomplish a similar objective: settling the mind so that it can experience its quieter states. Rabbi Shefa Gold is one of our leading teachers of chanting for transformative spiritual growth.[30] She describes three parts of a chant: setting one's intention prior to the chant; giving more and more at each repetition; and experiencing the silence afterwards. It is in the silence that Rabbi Gold says she receives the benefit of her practice—"a door opens . . . and in the silence I can walk through the door."[31]

Repeating a phrase, even if it is not chanted, also quiets the mind. Rabbi Nachman of Breslov taught that repeating the phrase "*Ribbono shel Olam*" (Master of the Universe) is a way to bring a person into a higher state of consciousness.[32] At first, the mind focuses on the literal meaning of the phrase. After a while, the literal meaning may fade away, giving rise to an emotion, or a subtler impulse, behind the phrase. Perhaps a sense of the vibration of the phrase is all that remains to resonate with the body and the mind, to bring them to a quieter level. The vibrations of a meaningless phrase, if properly chosen and utilized, also have the ability to resonate with the physiology, permitting the mind and body to slow down, experience quieter states, and perhaps transcend, to touch the quietest state.

---

30. Rabbi Gold's website can be found at www.rabbishefagold.com.
31. Waxman, "Chanting," 15:19—17:33.
32. Kaplan, *Jewish Meditation*, 57.

•   •   •

In these brief descriptions of a few meditation practices, I have characterized them as distinct techniques so that I could define and clarify each one more precisely. Yet, as I mentioned in the context of visualizations and concentration, these techniques are not mutually exclusive, and can sometimes be used together. Some of them rely on similar concepts, and the lines between them can become blurred. For example, in describing nullification (*bitul*) meditation, I described how the sages used visualizations of blackness or emptiness as a means to invite one's attention away from one's ego towards one's essence of *Ayin*, no-thingness.

Meditation Techniques In Contemporary Times

Rabbi Chaim Vital, considered a brilliant Kabbalist, was, for a period of about two years, a disciple of Rabbi Isaac Luria, the Ari. Were it not for Rabbi Vital, who was a prodigious author, many of the teachings of the Ari would not have been captured in writing. One of Rabbi Vital's primary works was a textbook on kabbalistic meditation called *Shaarey Kedushah* (Gates of Holiness). The fourth section of this book, describing specific methods of meditation that were ascribed to various sages, was never published, though a few manuscripts are said to exist.[33] There are several reasons that have been given for this: the sages believed that many of these powerful forms of meditation were to be reserved for the pious few; they needed to be taught face-to-face rather than through a book; and they were difficult and dangerous if not practiced correctly.[34]

Because many of our ancient practices have become obscured over time, they may be currently lost and unavailable to us.

33. Kaplan, *Meditation and Kabbalah*, 187–88, 190. On page 316, note 12, Kaplan references Part Four of the manuscript (Manuscript #749), indicating its presence in the British Museum.

34. Kaplan, *Meditation and Kabbalah*, 219; Kaplan, *Jewish Meditation*, 85–87, 91.

I expect that their secrets will be revealed to us again as our collective level of spiritual sophistication continues to grow and evolve. Contemporary teachers are rediscovering and adapting some of these practices to make them available to modern-day seekers.

The connection between meditative practice and the goal of Jewish meditation—touching the transcendent, unification with God—may not be immediately apparent to many modern-day practitioners. If we are concentrating on an object or thought, we are not letting go and returning to *Ayin*, to no-thingness. If we are focusing on our breath or becoming aware of our thoughts and emotions through a self-awareness exercise, we are not transcending. (Nonetheless, in both of the above cases, we very well may be calming down and/or gaining other valuable insights into our psyche.) But even if a meditation practice does not directly facilitate transcending, transcendence can still happen. Recall Dr. Gefen's description of the "open space" that can arise around the single point on which the meditator is focusing, such that they feel themselves becoming one with the Holy and the separate self is dissolving into a state of nonduality. Or think of the third part of Rabbi Gold's chanting process, in which a door opens, and in the silence she can walk through the door. Or think of how the mind, as a "mindfulness" meditation teacher described it to me, sometimes just lets go of everything and the experience becomes one of "mindlessness," or transcendence.

There are a number of modern meditation techniques. While it is not the purpose of this book to explore these in detail, I do provide a few suggestions in the afterword, as mentioned above, for those who wish to explore meditation further.

Chapter 5

Effects of Connection with the Transcendent

AN IMPORTANT THEME OF this book is that the *Ein Sof*, the hidden God, is our essence, and the essence of everything in creation. If our universe, metaphorically, is represented by a tree, then the *Ein Sof* is the sap of that tree. We are in the habit of sending our attention outward, to see and interact with the separate-looking aspects of life—the branches, leaves, flowers, and fruit of existence—not always recognizing that those differences are all only a disguise for their common essence: the sap. But when our minds touch (or better yet, cleave to) the level of the sap, deep in our awareness, then we see from "God's point of view." When our awareness becomes active at that level, we tap into the infinite intelligence that grows, nourishes, and integrates all components of the tree. And our thoughts, and therefore our actions, spontaneously reflect that universal perspective.

Should we, therefore, expect good things to happen as we more regularly experience and act from "God's point of view"? Yes, and they do. In this chapter, we will explore a small number of the many hundreds of research efforts that have been undertaken over the last fifty years to show what happens in such cases. The results detailed below demonstrate the widespread benefits of transcending. To promote methodological consistency throughout the studies presented here, in this book I cite only scientific research studies specifically using the meditation practice Transcendental Meditation®.[1]

• • •

In the introduction to this book, after recounting my experience that "the world is unfolding just as it should be," I took a brief detour to acknowledge that while that statement is true, it is also true, *at the same time*, that the world is broken and we need to work to repair it. Here, again, I must make sure to acknowledge the complexity of this world. Am I stating that once we start regularly enlivening our connection with the *Ein Sof* (walking in God's ways), *only* good things will happen to us in life, all our problems, issues, and health conditions will immediately resolve? Unfortunately, that is not the case. We all carry some baggage, some history, some consequences of past decisions that affect our current and future situations. Not only that, but random events can also occur that may knock us off balance. To make the situation even more complicated, Torah teaches that the iniquities of the parents are visited upon the children, and the children's children, to the third and fourth generations (Exod 20:5, 34:7, Num 14:18). This is hard for most of us to accept, and brings up the issue of theodicy, how to explain evil and suffering in the world; I will address this topic briefly in chapter 6.

But in spite of these stumbling blocks that all of us experience along the path of life, Moses reiterates, in his final exhortations to the Israelites, that blessings will accrue to them if they follow God's commandments, and curses will ensue if they do not (Deut

1. Transcendental Meditation® is a transcending-oriented form of meditation, taught using a consistent methodology, that has been practiced around the world since the late 1950s. As a result, hundreds of scientific studies of this practice have been conducted at respected institutions and/or published in peer-reviewed journals.

27–28). From a Jewish point of view, doing the right thing, walking in God's ways, makes a difference. So it's worth doing our best, even though we can't guarantee results.

Individual Effects

In this section, I detail numerous scientifically proven effects of transcending, according to hundreds of careful studies that have been carried out over the last five decades. References to the studies themselves can be found in the notes, with details in the bibliography. For clarity and ease of understanding, I have grouped the scientific studies around transcending into three major kinds of effects: mind/body rest and integration, health and physical improvements, and mental and psychological benefits.

Mind/Body Rest and Integration

When the mind settles, the body also rests. This shows up in many different ways:

- Brain-wave activity demonstrates distinctive patterns: the coexistence of theta and delta waves (indicating rest) with high-amplitude alpha and beta waves (indicating alertness) and the high synchronicity (coherence) of brain wave activity between the front and back of the brain.[2]

- Decreased blood flow to the kidneys and liver, along with increased blood flow to the brain, further indicates physiological rest coexisting with mental alertness.[3]

- Decreased sweat gland activity (increased basal skin resistance) indicates rest.[4]

2. Hebert and Lehmann, "Theta Bursts"; Rouzeré et al., "High Amplitude Fronto-Central Alpha"; Wallace et al., "Wakeful Hypometabolic Physiologic State"; Banquet, "Spectral Analysis"; Banquet, "EEG and Meditation."

3. Jevning et al., "Alterations in Blood Flow"; Jevning et al., "Redistribution of Blood Flow."

4. Laurie, "Investigation into the Changes"; West, "Changes in Skin

- Decreased oxygen consumption and respiratory rate (number of breaths per minute) are additional markers of rest. Breathing is occasionally spontaneously suspended, with no hyperventilation afterwards to compensate.[5]

- Muscles relax.[6] Cortisol, the stress hormone, decreases.[7] Lactate, a metabolic waste by-product, is reduced, signifying an overall slowing down of the metabolic system.[8]

Taken together, these changes point to a unique physiological state, characterized by measurements that are distinct from those taken during waking, dreaming, or sleeping. This state is characterized as a state of "restful alertness," in which the body is resting deeply while, at the same time, the mind is alert.[9] But to what is the mind alert? It is alert to "no-thingness," to *Ayin*. There is a cessation of thoughts, feelings, and input from the senses.

The participants whose physiological markers are being measured are asked to signal when they realize that they are no longer *not* thinking any thoughts (i.e. when they have once again begun to think thoughts). They cannot signal when they are not thinking or feeling, because they are not thinking at that time. The researchers then look at the physiological markers that were recorded immediately preceding the participant's signal. Prior to the signal, the breath slowed or was suspended; heart rate decreased. Subjectively, the participants reported having experienced a sense of inner wakefulness, loss of a sense of time, unboundedness, and/or calm during those periods when they were not thinking or

---

Resistance."

5. Allison, "Respiratory Changes"; Wallace and Benson, "Physiology of Meditation"; Farrow and Hebert, "Breath Suspension"; Severide, "Physiological and Phenomenological Aspects."

6. Jevning et al., "Muscle and Skin Blood Flow"; Kemmerling, "Wirkung."

7. Subrahmanyam and Porkodi, "Neurohumoral Correlates"; Bevan et al., "Endocrine Changes."

8. Wallace and Benson, "Physiology of Meditation"; Jevning et al., "Plasma Prolactin and Cortisol."

9. Wallace, "Physiological Effects"; Wallace et al., "Wakeful Hypometabolic Physiologic State"; Wallace and Benson, "Physiology of Meditation."

feeling.[10] During that same time, the coherence of brainwave patterns across the brain was stronger.[11] All of these markers indicate an experience of transcendence.

Over time, with repetition, these physiological and subjective experiences become integrated into a person's normal functioning. In the laboratory, longer-term meditators demonstrate increased brain wave coherence even when they are not meditating.[12] And in these same longer-term meditators, the alpha brain wave pattern and coherence across the brain have been shown to continue outside of meditation—even when the subjects are asked to focus on particular activities or when they are asleep. Subjectively, these individuals report an unbroken sense of alertness, or awareness, along with their normal activities while awake, as well as when they are dreaming or sleeping.[13] *This is cleaving to God.*

Earlier in this book, I quoted Rabbi Abraham Joshua Heschel as he described the piety of such an individual: "With his heart open to and attracted by some spiritual gravitation, the pious man moves, as it were, toward the center of a universal stillness, and his conscience is so placed as to listen to the voice of God."[14]

And how do the meditators themselves subjectively describe this experience, this ongoing experiencing of universal stillness even outside of meditation? Not surprisingly, some of them have written eloquently and profoundly about what happens in their awareness.

- "The underlying field of pure awareness remains unchanged whether going into or coming out of sleeping, dreaming, or waking—always unchanged, unperturbed, unaltered, with no detectable transition[15] . . . I could no longer speak of fall-

10. Severide, "Physiological and Phenomenological Aspects"; Travis and Pearson, "Pure Consciousness."

11. Haynes et al., "Psychophysiology of Advanced Participants."

12. Travis, "Eyes Open"; Travis et al., "Patterns of EEG Coherence."

13. Mason et al. "Electrophysiological Correlates"; Travis et al., "Patterns of EEG Coherence"; Travis, "Transcendental Experiences"; Travis et al., "Psychological and Physiological Characteristics."

14. Heschel, "Moral Grandeur and Spiritual Audacity," 308.

15. Pearson, *Supreme Awakening*, 500.

ing asleep. That phrase doesn't fit the reality. Now I *fall awake*. The difference is subtle but real. When one falls awake, one loses awareness of the body but not the wakefulness of pure awareness[16] . . . So many times each day I notice that things just get taken care of[17] . . . Life gets richer. And it's all just that because we are now more in the flow of nature, of cosmic life. We no longer experience ourselves as somehow outside of nature."[18]

- "The flurry of waking activity comes and goes; the inertia of sleep comes and goes. Yet, throughout these changing values of waking and sleeping, there is a silent, unbounded continuum of awareness that is me; I am never lost to myself."[19]

- "At first pure consciousness is experienced more as a backdrop to these changing states, a kind of screen against which all other things are experienced. But as it grows stronger, this abiding experience of pure awareness ultimately *eclipses* waking, dreaming, and sleeping, which comprise what we thought of as living."[20]

- "I experience myself as both being connected to and an expression of Infinity, or more precisely, what I experience as a brilliant spark of that Infinity which I feel we all are."[21]

- "I could really feel an absolute divine reality, where everything is seen in terms of bliss and unity. When I took a walk, I could really feel wholeness in everything. I would step on the ground and feel like the world had a heart which was pumping at the same time as mine, giving me an amazing feeling of unity."[22]

16. Pearson, *Supreme Awakening*, 500.

17. Pearson, *Supreme Awakening*, 512.

18. Pearson, *Supreme Awakening*, 512.

19. Travis et al., "Patterns of EEG Coherence," 4662.

20. Pearson, Supreme Awakening, 500.

21. Nader, *One Unbounded Ocean*, 186.

22. Nader, *One Unbounded Ocean*, 194–95.

- "Boundaries start to dissolve, and the outside is starting to feel part of me. The trees reflect my bliss and seem part of me, colors are deep and bright. Details are clear. Spontaneous knowledge comes into my mind. I feel attuned with God."[23]

Many years ago, I had a hint of such an experience. It was not as profound as the ones described above, and it came from the opposite direction—realizing I had a sense of connection with everything around me only after having lost it. It was after about one year of meditation, and things seemed to be going more smoothly in my life. Sure, problems appeared every day, but they worked themselves out, and they seemed to do so with less effort on my part. It wasn't anything in particular that I could put my finger on. I remember thinking to myself, "Things are going pretty well. I wonder if I need to keep meditating?" So I stopped and didn't think much about it. And I remember coming home from work a week later, frazzled, and plopping down on the couch. I'll never forget the image that flashed into my mind. "I feel like I'm one of those hamsters running around in an exercise wheel. I am running faster and faster, getting more and more tired, and I don't seem to be accomplishing anything." I paused for a moment to realize what I had just said to myself. Then I remembered that I had not been meditating for a week. I started up again and have not stopped since. When my awareness regularly touches the shared essence of all existence, it causes me to be *aligned with*, rather than *at odds with*, the world around me.

The experiences recounted above were written by individuals who had been transcending regularly over the years, cultivating the long-term integration of *Ayin* into their awareness. But anyone, at any time, can find themself fleetingly experiencing the transcendent—and sometimes the experience is more than fleeting. After all, it is the essence of all of us: it is not outside of us; we are never not connected to it. It is just that for many of us, the awareness of that essence and that connection has faded into the background.

---

23. Nader, *One Unbounded Ocean*, 195.

Across the millennia, countless individuals from all walks of life—saints, poets, religious leaders, writers, politicians, musicians, scientists, actors—have described such experiences. In 1902, William James collected accounts of this kind of experience in his book *The Varieties of Religious Experience*. A more recent and accessible compendium of transcendental experiences can be found in Dr. Craig Pearson's *The Supreme Awakening*.

The message I want to convey to my readers here is that we do not have to just wait around, hoping that we might randomly fall into such experiences. Our sages teach us that we can—and more precisely, that we are in fact commanded to—actively pursue, bring to the foreground, and stabilize this state of attachment with God.

Health and Physical Improvements

The resting and integration of the mind and body result in many health and physical improvements. Blood pressure decreases.[24] In patients with coronary artery disease, cardiovascular functioning improves.[25] Reaction times become faster.[26] Athletic performance improves.[27] Individuals' biological age (measured by auditory threshold, near-point vision, and systolic blood pressure) decreases compared to their chronological age.[28] Other measures of aging also decrease as individuals enjoy improved mental health, increased cognitive flexibility, increased learning ability, greater

24. Benson and Wallace, "Decreased Blood Pressure"; Cooper and Aygen, "Effect of Transcendental Meditation"; Wallace et al., "Systolic Blood Pressure and Long-Term Practice."

25. Zamarra et al., "Usefulness of the Transcendental Meditation Program."

26. Wandhofer et al., "Shortening of Latencies"; Holt et al., "Transcendental Meditation vs Pseudo-Meditation"; Banquet and Lesèvre, "Event-Related Potentials"; Cranson et al., "P300 Under Conditions of Temporal Uncertainty."

27. Reddy et al., "Effects of the Transcendental Meditation"; Reddy, "Role of the Transcendental Meditation."

28. Wallace et al., "Effects of the Transcendental Meditation"; Toomey et al., "Transcendental Meditation."

behavioral flexibility, and a greater sense of well-being.[29] Less recourse is had to medical care, and medical costs decrease.[30] Both prescription and non-prescription drug use, including cigarette smoking, decrease.[31] For the elderly with hypertension, mortality rates are lowered.[32]

Mental and Psychological Benefits

As the mind and body settle and health and physical improvements occur, a wide range of mental and psychological benefits also accrue to the practitioners. Their intelligence and cognitive performance improve, and neuroticism decreases.[33] Their self-confidence, inner-directedness, and self-actualization increase.[34] Their anxiety and depression, including symptoms of post-traumatic stress disorder (PTSD), decrease.[35] Their empathy,

29. Alexander et al., "Effects of the Transcendental Meditation"; Alexander et al., "Transcendental Meditation, Mindfulness, and Longevity."

30. Herron et al., "Cost-Effective Hypertension Management"; Herron and Hillis, "Impact of the Transcendental Meditation."

31. Browne et al., "Improved Mental and Physical Health"; Royer, "Role of the Transcendental Meditation."

32. Barnes et al., "Impact of Transcendental Meditation"; Schneider et al., "Long-Term Effects of Stress Reduction."

33. Tjoa, "Meditation, Neuroticism and Intelligence"; Aaron et al., "Transcendental Meditation Program"; Kotchabhakdi et al., "Improvement of Intelligence"; Cranson et al., "Transcendental Meditation and Improved Performance"; So and Orme-Johnson, "Three Randomized Experiments"; Dixon et al., "Accelerating Cognitive and Self-Development"; Nidich et al., "Effect of the Transcendental Meditation."

34. Seeman et al., "Influence of Transcendental Meditation"; Hjelle, "Transcendental Meditation and Psychological Health"; Nystul and Garde, "Comparison of Self-Concepts"; Dillbeck et al., "Longitudinal Effects"; Alexander et al., "Transcendental Meditation"; Chandler et al., "Transcendental Meditation Program"; Travis et al., "Psychological and Physiological Characteristics."

35. Dillbeck, "Effect of the Transcendental Meditation"; Stern, "Effects of the Transcendental Meditation"; Ferguson and Gowan, "TM–Some Preliminary Psychological Findings"; Travis et al., "Psychological and Physiological Characteristics"; Brooks and Scarano, "Transcendental Meditation"; Nidich et al., "Non-Trauma-Focused Meditation"; Bellehsen et al., "Pilot Randomized

sociability, acceptance, and positivity increase.[36] Their recidivism decreases.[37] Their moral reasoning improves.[38] And their creativity increases.[39]

The studies above (as well as many others not cited here) represent thousands of hours of empirical measurements, conducted over dozens of years, using standard, professionally-accepted assessment tools. The results that they present are statistically significant, having eliminated other variables that might have affected the outcomes. In other words, these are not just anecdotes. The track record of broad-based healing that is derived from repeated experiences of transcending, reported from multiple perspectives, cannot be ignored.

It can sometimes feel surprising to people to learn that a spiritual experience and practice could have such sturdy measurable effects on our physical bodies. So what is going on here? The practice of transcending immerses our entire being in God's infinite light. It is the nature of our physical bodies (and indeed of the physical environment in general) to break down.[40] But by reconnecting with God and recharging ourselves in the field of infinite orderliness and intelligence that governed and continues to govern our creation, we are repaired. In fact, looking at it this way, it would actually be surprising if tapping into this field did *not* heal us at all levels.

Controlled Trial."

36. Griggs, "Preliminary Study"; Hanley and Spates, "Transcendental Meditation"; Gelderloos et al., "Cognitive Orientation"; Sridevi and Krishna Rao, "Temporal Effects."

37. Alexander et al., "Effects of the Transcendental Meditation"; Bleick, "Influence of the Transcendental Meditation."

38. Nidich, "Study of the Relationship"; Kotchabhakdi et al., "Improvement of Intelligence"; Nidich and Nidich, "Transcendental Meditation and TM-Sidhi Program"; Nidich and Nidich, "Empirical Study"; Chandler et al., "Transcendental Meditation Program."

39. Travis, "Creative Thinking"; Jedrczak et al., "TM-Sidhi Program."

40. Lucas, "Second Law of Thermodynamics," lines 1-6.

Group Effects

What about group effects? Can the experience of one person transcending have an effect on another person? Yes. Using the phrase "returning [to *Ha-Shem*]" to mean praying, or returning to God, Rabbi Pinchas of Koretz (1726–1791), a disciple of the Baal Shem Tov, taught that:

> *Ha-Shem*, may He be blessed, is the sum of all souls. Everything that pertains to the whole is also found in a part. Consequently, what is related to one soul pertains to all the souls and therefore when you yourself return [to *Ha-Shem*], as a result of this even your friend returns [to *Ha-Shem*]—for he is included in his colleague and his colleague is included in him.[41]

Dr. Mark Verman teaches, "By connecting with *Ha-Shem* during meditation, you are involving *Ha-Shem* in a communion with all humanity."[42]

And what about the wider world? Can the mental and physical coherence of a relatively small number of individuals propagate and produce a positive effect on society as a whole? Torah says yes to this as well.[43] As we discussed in chapter 3, when God tells Abraham that he is going to destroy Sodom and Gomorrah, Abraham convinces God to spare the entire cities if there are as few as ten righteous individuals in them. God says, "I will not destroy, for the sake of the ten" (Gen 18:32). Apparently, had there been ten, their virtue would have been sufficient to avert the destruction of the many.

In Talmud (b. Sanh. 97b). "Abaye said: The world has no fewer than thirty-six righteous people in each generation who greet the Divine Presence." Legend has it that the simple presence of these righteous individuals (*tzaddikim*) is enough to hold up the world, keeping it from disintegrating into chaos. In Yiddish,

---

41. Verman, *History and Varieties of Jewish Meditation*, 26, referencing Midrash Pinchas, no 21, 13b.

42. Verman, *History and Varieties of Jewish Meditation*, 26.

43. Thanks to Bob Rabinoff for highlighting these examples to me.

they are called the "*lamedvovniks*," for the Hebrew letters *lamed*, signifying 30, and *vav*, signifying 6.

When the Israelites "follow [God's] laws and faithfully observe [God's] commandments," Torah tells us, "Five of you shall give chase to a hundred, and a hundred of you shall give chase to ten thousand; your enemies shall fall before you by the sword" (Lev 26:3, 8).

And can we see the effects of this exponential power of the good even in modern times? Apparently so. There have been dozens of studies done that show the positive societal effects of a few people transcending. In the following, I describe a few of those studies.

The first study of the effects of a small number of people transcending together and positively affecting their environment was performed in 1976. Crime statistics for the years 1967 through 1973 from 11 small experimental cities, and 11 small control cities with similar demographics, from around the midwestern United States were analyzed. From 1967 to 1971, crime increased in all 22 cities. Over the course of 1972, individuals in the experimental cities received instruction in transcending meditation. By the end of 1972, a critical mass of the population in the experimental cities (1 percent of the population) was regularly meditating for twenty minutes twice a day. From 1972 to 1973, the crime rates in these experimental cities decreased by an average of 8.2 percent. In the control cities, on the other hand, they continued their rise, increasing by an average of 8.3 percent. These changes are statistically significant.[44] Another, larger, study, of 24 experimental and 24 control cities, produced similar statistically significant results.[45]

In 1978, a critical mass of meditators was sent to five trouble spots around the world: Nicaragua, Lebanon, Iran, Cambodia, and Zimbabwe (then called Rhodesia). Data from the Conflict and Peace Data Bank shows that during the period that the meditators

44. Borland and Landrith, "Improved Quality of City Life."
45. Dillbeck and Landrith, "Transcendental Meditation Program."

were present, cooperative events increased and verbal hostilities and the number of hostile acts decreased.[46]

During a six-week period in 1979, a larger group of transcending meditators gathered in Amherst, Massachusetts; this group was apparently large enough to influence not only the state, but the country as well. Compared to the same six-week period in the previous several years, the decrease of violent crimes was statistically significant, as were the decreases in traffic, air, and overall fatalities, including fatalities due to accidents, suicides, and homicides. And in each of the two following years (1980 and 1981), when the group was no longer assembled, those numbers rose again.[47]

Another study tracked the size of coherence-creating groups in Lebanon and Israel during August and September of 1983. The intensity of war and the number of war deaths in Lebanon decreased, as did crimes, auto accidents, and other negative indicators in Israel. Positive indicators, such as the Israeli national stock index, increased.[48]

In late December of 1983 and early January of 1984, an even larger group (numbering approximately 7,000 people) gathered in Iowa. The coherence that was thereby generated at this larger scale improved social indicators worldwide. After the group dispersed, indicators declined again. These indicators included: increased progress made by heads of state around the world in reversing negative trends and accelerating positive ones (based on content from the New York Times); a significant shift towards greater positivity in events in global trouble spots (as measured by the International Conflict Scale); increased progress towards peaceful resolution of the Lebanese conflict (based on content from Al Nahar, a major Lebanese newspaper); and rising world stock indices (based upon data in the Wall Street Journal).[49]

---

46. Orme-Johnson et al., "Experimental Analysis."
47. Davies and Alexander, "Maharishi Technology."
48. Orme-Johnson et al., "International Peace Project."
49. Orme-Johnson et al., "Influence of the Maharishi Technology."

Finally, beginning in August of 1984, a group of approximately fifteen hundred participants came together in Manila, Philippines. Over the following five months, the number of participants varied. Through a time-series impact assessment, it was demonstrated that when the number of participants increased enough to surpass a critically large number, crime levels decreased. When the number of transcending participants decreased below that number, crime levels increased.[50]

•   •   •

Can we discern any scientific principles that might underlie what is happening in all of these cases? Perhaps. There are several that may point us in the direction of an explanation.

One principle is the power of wave coherence. Let us explore the science behind how a laser (light amplification by stimulated emissions of radiation) works. With a conventional light source, the light is a consequence of photons being emitted in a random manner. This results in radiation of different wavelengths, moving in different directions at different times, and producing a light of relatively low intensity. A laser, on the other hand, releases photons of the same wavelength, moving in the same direction, at exact time intervals. This coherence of a relatively small number of photons produces an multiplicative (or amplified per its acronym) intensity of light far surpassing that which would be produced by the same number of photons from a conventional (incoherent) light source.[51] This phenomenon supports the idea that wave coherence (and in the case of meditators, brain wave coherence) greatly amplifies the ability of a small number (of photons, or of meditators) to affect their surroundings.

Another potentially useful principle is the concept of superconductivity as a way to repel disorder. Normally, as a substance cools, its resistance to an electrical current passing through it is reduced in a linear fashion with the temperature. However, as

50. Dillbeck et al., "Consciousness as a Field."

51. "Lasers," paras. 3, 4.

explained on the website for the European Council for Nuclear Research (CERN):

> Below a certain "critical" temperature, materials undergo transition into the superconducting state, characterized by two basic properties: firstly, they offer no resistance to the passage of electrical current. When resistance falls to zero, a current can circulate inside the material without any dissipation of energy. Secondly, provided they are sufficiently weak, external magnetic fields will not penetrate the superconductor, but remain at its surface. This field expulsion phenomenon is known as the Meissner effect, after the physicist who first observed it in 1933.[52]

Thus, the slowing down (or "cooling down") of an individual's physiology described above (e.g., their suspension of breath) may be analogous to the cooling of a material, to the point where outside influences of disorder will not penetrate (field expulsion).

Then, there is the existence of quantum entanglement, which Albert Einstein famously called "spooky action at a distance." As the science journalist Zeeya Merali writes in the journal *Nature*:

> In quantum mechanics, objects can be in multiple states simultaneously: for example, an atom can be in two places, or spin in opposite directions, at once. Measuring an object forces it to snap into a well-defined state. Furthermore, the properties of different objects can become "entangled," meaning that their states are linked: when a property of one such object is measured, the properties of all its entangled twins become set, too. This idea galled Einstein because it seemed that this ghostly influence would be transmitted instantaneously between even vastly separated but entangled particles—implying that it could contravene the universal rule that nothing can travel faster than the speed of light.[53]

52. CERN. "Superconductivity," para. 2.

53. Merali, "Quantum 'Spookiness,'" paras. 4–5.

This phenomenon supports the idea that the coherence of individuals in one location might affect the coherence of others, even at great distances.

Bruce Russett, the editor of the *Journal of Conflict Resolution*, a peer-reviewed journal in which the Israel/Lebanon study cited above was published, was at a loss to explain the results. He wrote, "This hypothesis has no place within the normal paradigm of conflict and peace research. Yet this hypothesis seems logically derived from the initial premises and its empirical testing seems competently executed." The methodology was further scrutinized, and the authors submitted a revised version of the paper "in which methodological problems with the original seemed to have been properly addressed." The paper was sent out to external reviewers, as is standard practice. One external reviewer stated that the paper "has a great deal of merit, in that the author(s) proceeds to examine a hypothesis that is on (or just beyond) the fringe of accepted 'scientific knowledge' in a very professional fashion." Another characterized it as "a logically and methodologically coherent effort to test a set of hypotheses that, to be blunt, I regard as absurd." The bottom line is that the journal did publish the paper, with Russett noting that "Galileo was censored because his views offended the precepts of religious authorities."[54] Apparently, Russett did not want to practice the modern equivalent of that kind of censorship.

No detailed, comprehensive scientific explanation of what is happening in these situations is available to us at this time. The scientific principles I have just cited are simply pointers towards possible explanations that may be contributing to the results being measured. Nonetheless, these empirical successes should cause us to continue to try to replicate these experiments and develop a deeper understanding of these phenomena. We are breaking boundaries and entering into a new age.

54. Russett, "Editor's Comment."

Chapter 6

Transcendental Judaism and Implications for the Messianic Age

FOR JEWS, THE MESSIANIC age, not yet arrived, is traditionally characterized as a time when the Temple will be rebuilt in Jerusalem, Jewish exiles will be brought back to the land of Israel, evil and sin will be no more, there will be widespread awareness and knowledge of God, the world will experience peace and harmony, the dead will be resurrected, and there will be an end to disease and death.[1] Let's review some biblical texts that describe this messianic age in more detail.

The Temple Is Rebuilt

"I will place my Sanctuary among them forever. My Presence shall rest over them . . . My Sanctuary abides among (within) them forever" (Ezek 37:26–28). Not only does the "Sanctuary" refer to the Temple being physically rebuilt, but "My Presence" and "My Sanctuary" also refer to the awareness of God's presence among and within the people, as a result of their experiences of transcendence and their

1. Schochet, "Messianic Era."

ability to cleave to God. This is reinforced by the wording in Torah at the time of the building of the *mishkan*, the portable tabernacle that traveled with the Hebrews in the desert prior to the construction of the Temple: "And let them make Me a sanctuary that I may dwell among them" (Exod 25:8). Torah does not say that God will dwell in the *mishkan*, but that God will dwell among the people.

The Exiles Return

Isaiah 43:5–6 is often quoted in support of the literal return of the exiles: "I will bring your folk from the East, will gather you out of the West; I will say to the North, 'Give back!' and to the South, 'Do not withhold!' Bring My sons from afar, and My daughters from the end of the earth."

But let us not forget the immediate lead-up to this passage (Isa 43:1–2): "Fear not, for I will redeem you . . . When you pass through water, I will be with you; through streams, they shall not overwhelm you. When you walk through fire, you shall not be scorched; through flame, it shall not burn you." Who or what is the "you" to whom God is referring here, the "you" that will be redeemed and not be drowned or burned? It is the transcendent, hidden "you" that will be redeemed and returned from exile— brought from the background to the foreground of our awareness—so that we realize that the true essence of ourselves is the indestructible, ever-present *Ein Sof*.

Evil and Sin Are No More

"In those days and at that time—declares the LORD—the iniquity of Israel shall be sought and there shall be none; the sins of Judah, and none shall be found" (Jer 50:20). This supports the trends described in chapter 5 that document an increase in moral reasoning and reduced crime because of our practice of enlivening the Eternal within us.

Widespread Awareness and Knowledge of God

"For the earth shall be filled with awe for the glory of the LORD as water covers the sea" (Hab 2:14).[2] This reinforces the teaching that "the world is God, wrapped in robes of God so as to appear to be material." In messianic times, the godliness in everything will shine forth in our awareness. (The godliness shines now as well; we are just not often aware of it.) We will be able to see both from "our point of view" (in other words, seeing objects, people, things) and from "God's point of view" (seeing the essential oneness that is the essence of all).

Peace and Harmony

"And they shall beat their swords into plowshares and their spears into pruning hooks. Nation shall not take up sword against nation; they shall never again know war" (Micah 4:3; Isaiah 2:4). This also supports the studies described in chapter 5 that document reductions in crime and in international violence.

The Dead Are Resurrected

"You shall know, O My people, that I am the LORD, when I have opened your graves and lifted you out of your graves. I will put My breath into you and you shall live again" (Ezek 37:13–14). The literal meaning of this passage is that bodies will be resurrected and will live on the earth again. But the word *ruach*, translated here as "breath," also means "spirit." A figurative interpretation of this promise of God's is that it refers to a time when we will become aware that the true essence of ourselves is indestructible. Though our bodies may die, we will know that the transcendental aspect of ourselves (and of everything in the universe) never dies.

2. Compare Isa 11:9: "For the land shall be filled with devotion to the LORD as water covers the sea."

An End to Disease and Death

"Then the eyes of the blind shall be opened, and the ears of the deaf shall be unstopped. Then the lame shall leap like a deer, and the tongue of the dumb shall shout aloud" (Isa 35:5–6). Again, this message points to the studies described in chapter 5 that document health and physical improvements.

• • •

All of these descriptions of a better society consistently match with the documented beneficial effects of individuals and groups transcending. But who or what brings about the messianic age? Traditionally, our texts teach that the messiah (*machiach*), a descendant of King David, will arise; that "the spirit of the LORD shall alight upon him: a spirit of wisdom and insight, a spirit of counsel and valor, a spirit of devotion and reverence for the LORD" (Isa 11:2); and that he will usher in the messianic age. Our more modern understanding is that as a result of the performance of meritorious activities and repentance by the people, the messiah will arrive. As Rabbi Green teaches, "The actual work of redeeming the world is turned to us in history, and is done by all of us, day by day . . . Only when redemption is about to be completed will messiah be allowed to arrive. *Rather than messiah redeeming us, we redeem messiah.*"[3] In other words, as we have seen again and again throughout this book, when we enliven the Eternal within us, we uplift ourselves and the world.

The God/Human Dynamic

Perhaps, then, it is we, through our actions, who usher in the messiah. In chapter 3, we noted a shift over time in the dynamic of God's control over events in the world—from God's complete control in the creation of the world, through Noah and many prophets following God's instructions exactly as given to them, then God

3. Green, *Seek My Face*, 179–80 (emphasis in original).

negotiating and compromising with Abraham and Moses over outcomes, and God changing the laws when people spoke up, to, finally, God being disregarded when trying to offer an opinion on a *halachic* ruling.

So does God control events in the world or do we? Let's explore this God/human dynamic through the lens of one of the themes of this book—nonduality, the recognition that there is nothing other than God, the world is simply God's garment. From this perspective, we might perceive that we and everything around us are aspects of the *Ein Sof*, clothed in our unique garments that reflect our unique combinations of attributes and capabilities.

If our essence is the *Ein Sof* , the transcendent, hidden God manifested in humans, then God may not be separate from us. And the answer to "who is acting?" may not be so clear. What if God is in fact acting (or not acting) through our own actions (and not only through our actions, but through all manifest phenomena)? When God tells Moses at the burning bush that God's name is *Ehyeh Asher Ehyeh* (I Shall Be As I Shall Be), perhaps that is God's way of saying, "We will see how I show up in the world. It depends, in large part, on what aspects of My infinite possibilities *you* (humankind) bring forth."

Rabbi Green reminds us that after World War II, when Rabbi Heschel was asked, "Where was God during the Holocaust?", his reply was, "That is the wrong question. 'Where was man?' is what we have to ask."[4] In the past, we have assumed that these were two different questions. But in the context of nonduality, we realize they are actually the exact same question: where were we in bringing forth the qualities of compassion and justice into the world?

The theology presented throughout this book is that "we are aspects of God acting in the world." Process Theology, a less radical theology than the one expounded here, nevertheless teaches a message that is largely consistent with this. It teaches that God is not omnipotent or unchanging but that we are in a dynamic, constantly co-creative relationship with God.[5] However, although

4. Green, *Judaism for the World*, 107.

5. Artson, *God of Becoming and Relationship*, 9–20.

it acknowledges that all of existence is God and is pervaded by divinity,[6] the language of Process Theology still largely presents God as an "other" with whom we "become together."

But even if we hold a much more traditional view, picturing a powerful and separate God residing in heaven, we still accept that we are created in the image of God and that our performance of the *mitzvot*, and our other actions, make a difference in the world.

In other words, then, no matter how we view the godliness within us, we understand both our actions and our failures to act contribute to the reality around us. As a tool for expanding our thinking, we can present these perspectives on the God/human dynamic as being on the following continuum:

The God/Human Dynamic

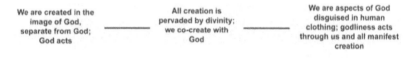

We are created in the image of God, separate from God; God acts	All creation is pervaded by divinity; we co-create with God	We are aspects of God disguised in human clothing; godliness acts through us and all manifest creation

• • •

And what about prayer, in this construction? When we pray to God, to whom are we praying? Often, prayer is something we do for ourselves: it comforts us, gives us hope, or enables us to alter our perspective on a situation. There is a deep truth in the Jewish saying, "Pray as if everything depended on God; act as if everything depended on you." Again, this blurs the line between God and us.

Rabbi Green has observed that "Every prayer we utter, every time we say the vital word 'You' in prayer, proclaiming God our beloved, we are also confirming our separation from the One that we hope would (and, on some level, *does*) embrace us all."[7] This

6. Artson, *God of Becoming and Relationship*, 15, referencing Cordovero, *Shiur Komah* to Zohar 3:14b as saying: "The essence of divinity is found in every single thing—nothing but it exists.... Do not say, 'This is a stone and not God.' God forbid! Rather all existence is God, and the stone is a thing pervaded by divinity."

7. Green, *Judaism for the World*, 285–86 (emphasis in original).

observation rings true to me, and it is troubling to me as well. How, then, should we pray? One potential answer to this conundrum is offered up by Rabbi Green himself, who teaches that God is transcendent and without attributes; that God has a thousand, a million, a billion faces that fill the world. As we have discussed above, our tradition teaches us that this is all the same God. So perhaps it is the One with a thousand, a million, a billion faces who hears when we call out "You."

It is not my aim here to try to reform our prayer liturgy in the light of transcendental Judaism. I only want to point out that it is worth examining the language that we use. Perhaps in the future, this language, too, or even the use of language in prayer at all, will evolve. In this context, we can remember Maimonides, who "taught that animal sacrifices were only commanded to the Jewish people as a concession, because it was the only type of Divine worship known in that era . . . that prayer was an evolution from animal sacrifice and a more silent, meditative type of worship will eventually supersede prayer with words."[8]

---

8. Yanklowitz, *Existing Eternally*, 144, interpreting Maimonides, "Guide for the Perplexed," pt. 3, ch. 32: "It was in accordance with the wisdom and plan of God, as displayed in the whole Creation, that He did not command us to give up and to discontinue all these manners of service [animal sacrifices]; for to obey such a commandment it would have been contrary to the nature of man, who generally cleaves to that to which he is used . . . As the sacrificial service is not the primary object [of the commandments about sacrifice], whilst supplications, prayers, and similar kinds of worship are nearer to the primary object, and indispensable for obtaining it, a great difference was made in the Law between these two kinds of service . . . We were not commanded to sacrifice in every place, and in every time, or to build a temple in every place, or to permit any one who desires to become priest and to sacrifice. On the contrary, all this is prohibited unto us . . . But prayer and supplication can be offered everywhere and by every person . . . Samuel therefore said, 'Hath the Lord as great delight in burnt-offerings and sacrifices as in obeying the voice of the Lord'? (1 Sam 15:22) . . . Jeremiah says [in the name of God] the primary object of the precepts is this, Know me, and serve no other being; 'I will be your God, and ye shall be my people' (Lev. 26:12) . . . The chief object of the Law, as has been shown by us, is the teaching of truths; to which the truth of the *creatio ex nihilo* belongs. "

The Question of Evil

As we push our thinking to the right along the continuum of perspectives on the God/human dynamic presented above, we might ask, when God acts through us, what are the attributes of God? We often think of God's attributes as the beneficent *sefirot* themselves: wisdom, lovingkindness, and beauty. But we know that when we act, we do not always manifest those attributes. So what about when we act from a place of selfishness, egotism, contempt, or evil? Are those attributes of God? If the essence of everything is God, it doesn't seem possible to argue that God's qualities are only good. This is the age-old question of theodicy: if God is good, why is there evil and suffering in the world?

Volumes have been and will continue to be written exploring the question of theodicy, from both religious and secular perspectives.[9] Although we cannot review all of that literature here, we can at least look to the Zohar for one perspective: a simple, elemental one that takes us to the moment of creation. After the first day, when God brought forth light, "God said, 'Let there be an expanse in the midst of the water, that it may separate water from water'" (Gen 1:6). The Zohar says about that act: "Here is mystery in detail, separating upper waters from lower through mystery of the left. Here conflict was created through the left side . . . Out of that conflict aroused by the left, emerged Hell."[10]

As we saw in chapter 2, the first emanation from the *Ein Sof* is *Chochmah* (on the right), a point of infinite wisdom "too fine and subtle to be detected without its reflections or reverberations in *Binah*"[11] (on the left). This introduction of another side (i.e., the left) is the introduction of duality itself, a necessary component of creation as we know it, but one that inevitably introduces differences, which enable conflict.

9. See Zuckier, "Traditional Jewish Approach." See also Kushner, *When Bad Things Happen*, for a number of explanations of evil and suffering.

10. Matt, *Zohar* 1:127–28.

11. Green, "Introduction," in Matt, *Zohar* 1:xlviii.

But all is not lost! Duality, and thus conflict, *do* become embedded as a part of creation (and as a part of God's "inner life," as we saw in chapter 2),[12] starting with the second day, when God separated water from water and the lower seven *sefirot* emanated from *Binah*.[13] And as we have just reviewed, that caused a conflict to arise between left and right. However, "the central pillar, who is the third day (*Tif'eret*), entered between them, mediating the conflict, reconciling the two sides. Hell descended, left merged in right, and peace prevailed over all."[14]

As we saw in chapter 2, the middle column of the *sefirot* balances the opposing qualities of the left and right columns. Here, *Tif'eret* is mediating the conflict, reconciling the two sides (*Chesed* or lovingkindness on the right and *Din* or judgment on the left). Importantly, when hell subsided, "left merged in right, and peace prevailed over all." This bears repeating: to create peace, right did not merge into left; it was left that merged into right. "Right is the consummate of all, so all is written by the right, for upon it depends all consummation."[15] So the overriding mediator of conflict (or hell) is the teaching that judgment is subsumed into lovingkindness.

• • •

Let us take another brief detour. I have been conflating duality with conflict. If there is oneness, there are no differences, and there is no place for conflict. But as soon as two options appear (e.g., ocean and dry land), distinctions must be made and dealt with. For instance, my wife might want blueberry pie for dessert, and I might want peach pie. We live our lives through the process of constructively working through the inevitability of duality in our world. (In the example above, we compromise and have blueberry pie!)

12. Green, "Introduction," in Matt, *Zohar* 1:xlvii.
13. Matt, *Zohar* 1:127–28n151.
14. Matt, *Zohar* 1:128 and 128n157.
15. Matt, *Zohar* 1:128.

But is it appropriate to conflate duality with evil? No, it is not. Duality makes the emergence of evil *possible*, but not *inevitable*. Duality descends into evil when people purposely make morally wicked choices such as promulgating violent crime, inflicting pain and suffering, or promoting falsehoods or injustice.[16]

But what about the pain and suffering caused by natural disasters? If God acts through all manifest creation, is God causing the famine, the tornado, or the pandemic? And if so, how . . . and why? God tells the Israelites (Lev 26:3–4), "If you follow My laws and faithfully observe My commandments, I will grant your rains in the season, so that the earth shall yield its produce and the trees of the field their fruit." But if God's commandments are not followed, "YHVH will make the rain of your land dust" (Deut 28:24) and "will make pestilence cling to you" (Deut 28:21).

Furthermore, Talmud (b. Sanh. 37b) teaches us that, at least in the case of the death penalty for individuals, the heavenly court intervenes in the world in place of the earthly court. In other words, if a person is guilty, but cannot be convicted to death by stoning because there were not two witnesses to the murder they committed, then an event will befall that person whereby they die a similar death (e.g., they fall from a roof and die of their broken bones).

We have made progress in understanding many laws of nature, particularly as they relate to sciences such as physics and chemistry. We can accurately predict the next eclipse, and we are confident that when we mix two parts hydrogen and one part oxygen, water will be the result. But do our societal behaviors affect outcomes in nature as well? In some cases, the link appears clear: if we leak toxins into the soil, crops will become contaminated and people in the vicinity will become ill. But to create a link between evil behavior and an earthquake, tornado, pandemic, or famine? Our current understanding of cause and effect in this world is nowhere sophisticated enough to be able to make a statement about that.

• • •

16. Cf. Matt, *God and the Big Bang*, 125: "Evil arises when someone is responsible for such acts as violent crime, military aggression, or genocide."

Rabbi Dr. Sid Schwarz reminds us that the sages taught that when we see evil existing, some of God is being obscured; that is the concept of *hester panim* (the hiding of the face of God) that we discussed earlier.[17] The attributes of God that are being obscured in that case are the attributes of lovingkindness, grace, and expansiveness. In the context of describing the balance between "the left" and "the right," Gershom Scholem writes: "The totality of divine potencies forms a harmonious whole, and as long as each stays in relation to all others, it is sacred and good."[18]

We need to make judgments and exercise power to function in the world. For example, one of our *mitzvot* tells us that we have the obligation to defend ourselves using force from a pursuer (*rodef*) who is trying to harm us (Deut 25:11–12). But our permitted use of force is not absolute and must be mediated by a broader understanding of the circumstances.[19]

How do we sustain in our awareness a balance of "the totality of divine potencies?" By going back to the source, immersing ourselves in the *Ein Sof*. That is the field where all is balanced, where opposites do not exist. Dov Baer (the Maggid of Mezeritch, ca. 1700/1710–1772), a disciple of the Baal Shem Tov, taught this message: "Think of yourself as *Ayin* and forget yourself totally. Then you can transcend time, rising to the world of thought, where all is equal: life and death, ocean and dry land."[20] It is from that place that balanced action will naturally arise.

Touching the Source Offers True Transformation

And it is that same source that makes true transformation possible. I have had the following experience: the tiniest thought impulse arises. I can hardly discern its content. As it continues to emerge, it

17. Schwarz, "Creation Story," at 1:18:00—1:20:15.

18. Scholem, *Major Trends in Jewish Mysticism*, 237.

19. Eisenberg, *613 Mitzvot*, 172.

20. Matt, "Online Zohar Course," "Reference: Ayin—No-thingness," 3, referencing Baer, *Maggid Devarav le-Ya'aqov*, 186; Matt, *Essential Kabbalah*, 71, 184.

takes shape; it begins to have substance. The more it emerges, the more concrete it becomes. But interestingly, I get the sense that, the more of a meaning it takes on, the more limited the possibilities become for its final outcome. It's like traveling down a funnel, starting at the wide end. Or a little bit like looking up a word in an online dictionary. Type in the first letter, and thousands of possible words are available. But then type the next letter, the next, and the one after that, and the list of possible outcomes rapidly decreases. When your word is fully spelled out, you have it, but you are then locked into it.

Now let's look at the same process, going backwards. Suppose that's not the word you meant. Delete a letter. Delete another. You will see more and more possible words appear, the further back you go. Your possibilities just keep increasing. Delete all the way back to your first letter and you now have more possibilities than you can see on one screen. You can switch to countless other words, but not an infinite number of them: you are still bound by the first letter you typed. Now delete that first letter. You are back at *Ayin*. You are locked into nothing, not even your initial impulse. You are completely free. Infinite possibilities, infinite transformation await you.

Daniel Matt writes that "nothingness [*Ayin*] embraces all potentiality."[21] He elaborates:

> it engenders new mental life, through a rhythm of annihilation and fresh thinking. As Dov Baer taught, "Turn away totally from the prior object of thought, toward a place called 'nothingness.' Then a new topic comes to mind. Transformation comes about only by passing through nothingness." In the words of one of his disciples, "When you attain the level of gazing at *Ayin*, your intellect is annihilated. Afterwards, when you return to the intellect, it is filled with emanation."[22]

21. Matt, *God and the Big Bang*, 63.

22. Matt, *God and the Big Bang*, 61. Matt, "Online Zohar Course," "Reference: Ayin—No-thingness," 4. For the source of this teaching, Matt cites the disciple of Dov Baer to whom he is referring in *God and the Big Bang*. It is Levi Yitzhak of Berditchev, quoted from *Qedushat Levi*, 71d.

And finally: "*Ayin* is the root of all things, and 'when you bring anything to its root, you can transform it. Each thing must first arrive at the level of *Ayin*; only then can it become something else.'"[23]

Unity Shines through Diversity

Throughout this book we have discussed the concept that the *Ein Sof* is the undifferentiated, unified source from which all diverse creation emerges. And we have argued that manifest creation is not separate from the *Ein Sof*. In fact, the *Ein Sof* is the living essence of all things in creation. In the Garden of Eden, Adam and Eve initially saw and experienced everything primarily as its essence—unity shone through diversity. It was only after they had eaten from the Tree of Knowledge of Good and Evil that duality overshadowed unity in their awareness. (And as we have discussed, this shift was a necessary one in order to introduce life in the multidimensional world outside of heaven/Eden.) We too have been conditioned to view separateness as our reality. And as we have seen, on one level, that separateness is real. But on a deeper level, oneness is real. Both of these truths exist at the same time; they need to, so that we can function in the world.

Can we live our lives without permitting the perception of diversity to overshadow the perception of unity? Can we let unity shine through diversity? In the early part of this book, I described my vivid experience of that phenomenon when, immediately after an experience of transcending, I knew that the birds in the trees and the cars on the highway were singing the song of life together in perfect harmony. Coming from the direct experience of the unity of the transcendent, my mind spontaneously applied that experience of unity to the objects of my outward attention. In other words, for an instant, the reality of unity began to shine through into my everyday perception of life as diversity. This was

23. Matt, *God and the Big Bang*, 62, referencing Dov Baer. Per Matt, "Online Zohar Course," "Reference: Ayin—No-thingness," 3, the reference is Baer, *Maggid Devarav le-Yaʾaqov*, 49, 91, 134.

how it happened for me. For each of us it will look a little different, but the common thread is that, as we saw in chapter 2 in the discussion of *devekut*—cleaving to God, repeated experiences of unity will stabilize themselves within our consciousness, so that we begin to be able to see and hold both sides of the coin at the same time.

Gershom Scholem taught:

> Originally, everything was conceived as one great whole, and the life of the Creator pulsated without hindrance or disguise in that of his creatures. Everything stood in direct mystical rapport with everything else, and its unity could have been apprehended directly and without the help of symbols. Only the Fall has caused God to become "transcendent." Its cosmic results have led to loss of the original harmonious union and to the appearance of an isolated existence of things . . . No wonder . . . the Kabbalists . . . describe the state of the Messianic world [as] . . . the restoration of the original coexistence and correlation of all things. What is at present reserved to the mystic whose gaze penetrates through the outer shell to the core of the matter, will anon be the common property of all mankind in the state of redemption.[24]

The prophet Zechariah pronounces, "On that day the LORD shall be one and [God's] name one" (Zech 14:9).[25] Now we understand this statement at a deeper level of meaning.

The contemporary meditation teacher Rabbi Jeff Roth teaches:

> Profane conduct is that which further reinforces our sense of separateness from other beings and from the Holy One of Being. Acting in holiness or sacredness would then be defined as cultivating the consciousness of the Interconnection of All Beings or All Being. In a reconceptionist approach, holiness is transformed from an expression of separateness from worldly matters to an

24. Scholem, *Major Trends in Jewish Mysticism*, 224.

25. As translated in Alter, *Hebrew Bible*, 2:1383. Sefaria's less widely recognized translation reads "in that day there shall be one Lord with one name."

expression of radical interconnection or non-separate-
ness. This flows from the realization that everything is
God and nothing but God.[26]

Rabbi Green adds to this, teaching that "our religious task is
to see through to the oneness of these two truths, to recognize that
the one beyond and the one within are the same One. We are then
charged to create a human community that lives and witnesses an
ongoing response to that insight."[27]

And that is the key, isn't it? Witnessing and living an ongoing
response to the insight that all things are originally one? We are
all one. And when our perception of the oneness of everything
shines through the perception that everything is different, then a
profound shift has occurred in our awareness. This is not just an
intellectual or emotional shift, but a life-changing experience of
the deepest truth of reality. Our actions will spontaneously adjust
to live this truth (*just as our actions now spontaneously reflect our
hit-and-miss ability to live this truth*). When we can regularly act
from the awareness of the interconnectedness of all beings, the
world will be a better place because of it.

Biblical and Rabbinic Judaism and the *Mitzvot* in the Era of Transcendental Judaism

In the introduction to this book, I described the *mitzvot* as the
backbone of Judaism, the constant that has informed and will
continue to inform our beliefs and actions throughout time. The
3,500-year history of Judaism is a long, evolutionary journey during which our pathways for connecting with God have become
ever broader and perhaps more easily attainable and sublime. As
we journey forward, we are not burning the bridges that previously connected us with God; instead, we are building additional
ones to broaden and enhance our paths of connection.

26. Roth, *Me, Myself and God*, 75–76.
27. Green, *Seek My Face*, 5.

In different eras, different *mitzvot* have been at the forefront of how we connected with God. In the early years, the *mitzvot* involving animal sacrifices played an outsize role in bringing our ancestors closer to God. Does that mean that in the future, a third Temple will be built and we will reinstitute the practice of animal sacrifices (as described in Leviticus 1:1—5:26—Parsha Vayikra— and elsewhere)? What about other Temple-related practices, such as sprinkling the ashes of a red heifer for ritual purification (Numbers 19:1–22—Parsha Chukat)? I certainly don't have answers to these questions. At the time of this writing, there are significant issues, geopolitical and other, that make the possibility of building a third Temple daunting. (Among other things: how would we ever find a completely red heifer? Perhaps through modern advances in bioengineering?) Some people are adamant that a third Temple must be built and these practices restored. Others are equally adamant that they should not. In terms of the subject matter of this book, the practice of quieting the mind and directly experiencing our transcendental nature neither supports nor detracts from the possibility of adding back these ancient rites. However, if they are indeed reinstituted, I believe that they will be viewed by most Jews as ceremonial and symbolic, rather than as integral ways of connecting with God.

Prior to the destruction of the second Temple, the religious leader and scholar Hillel (c. 110 BCE to 10 CE) summarized Torah's teachings as follows: "That which is hateful to you, do not do to another; that is the entire Torah, and the rest is its interpretation. Go study." (b. Šabb. 31a). Over the last two thousand years we have taken this teaching to heart, particularly embracing practices and *mitzvot* surrounding study, prayer, acts of charity, and repentance. These *mitzvot* will stay close to our hearts and will likely increase in practice as we, individually and as a society, cleave more closely to God.

In messianic times, which *mitzvot* will rise to prominence? Will Torah and the *mitzvot* evolve in some way, as I suggested in chapter 1? Or will it go further than evolution? Rav Yosef teaches (b. Nid. 61b) that the *mitzvot* will be nullified in the future. Why?

One interpretation of this statement is that in messianic times, we will be constantly living the word of God, and consequently, the *mitzvot* will no longer be needed. *Midrash* teaches that one day, God will expound to the righteous of the world about the new Torah that God will give to them by the hand of the messiah.[28] Concerning the Torah of the Messiah, Kohelet Rabbah (a commentary on Ecclesiastes) (11:8) teaches that the Torah a person learns in this world is *hevel*, compared with the Torah of the Messiah. *Hevel* is often translated as "futile," but a more accurate translation is "mere breath."[29] Rabbi Rami Shapiro teaches that the translation of *hevel* as "mere breath" connotes impermanence, something that is fleeting.[30] Applying this translation to the Torah of this world, we could say that we understand or experience it in our lives through the ever-changing nature of our manifest world—on the levels of *pshat* (literal meaning), *remez* (allegorical connection), and *drash* (the homiletical lesson), as we saw in chapter 3. In messianic times, we will integrate Torah into our lives on the level of unchanging permanence (*sod*), through the direct experience of the *Ein Sof*.

This idea is reinforced by the *Mei Hashiloach* (the thoughts and sermons of Rabbi Mordechai Leiner of Izbica, 1801–1854), through the interpretation of Rabbi Nathan Lopes Cardozo and the scholar Yehudah DovBer Zirkind:

> Torah and *mitzvot* are akin to garments whereby one can grasp God . . . but they do not constitute the unmediated and "naked" divine essence . . . This is analogous to a king and his royal garments. The royal garments reflect the glory and majesty of the king, but they are not identical

28. Matt, *Becoming Elijah*, 75, 176n77, quoting from *Otiyyot de Rabbi Aqiva* (The Alphabet of Rabbi Akiva) in Solomon Aaron Wertheimer, *Battei Midrashot*.

29. Matt, *Becoming Elijah*, 176n77.

30. Shapiro, *Ecclesiastes: Annotated and Explained*, xv. Rabbi Shapiro writes that in the defining opening words of Ecclesiastes, *hevel* is used not to mean that life is vain or futile but that it is transient and impermanent. "Ecclesiastes is a guidebook for living without permanence, surety, and security while still finding joy in living" (*Ecclesiastes: Annotated and Explained*, 2).

with the king himself. The *Mei Hashiloach* explains that, while in our current reality the only way to connect to God and [God's] will is through the garments of Torah and *mitzvot*, in the future there will be a direct revelation of Godliness without the mediation of garments.[31]

To put it in more concrete terms: in the future, the *mitzvot* that command us to directly experience and act from the unity of existence will guide our evolution. What are these *mitzvot*? They are the *mitzvot* to cleave to God and to love your neighbor as yourself, as well as the *mitzvah* related to repentance.[32] The Hebrew word for repentance, the act of feeling regret or contrition, is *teshuvah*, which carries the meaning of "return." When we repent, to what are we returning? We are returning to the wholeness of the *Ein Sof*, our true essence that we have never lost, but which has faded into the background of our awareness. We are returning to the embrace of God, the place from which balanced action arises, the place from which true transformation occurs, the place from which unity shines through diversity. When we transcend, that is the place to which we return. When we return there, we are healed, and then we go out and heal the world.

31. Zirkind, "Perfect Torah—part 3," paras. 17–18.

32. Eisenberg, *613 Mitzvot*. Eisenberg gives the examples of Numbers 5:6–7: "Any man or woman who commits any trespass against the Lord . . . shall confess their sin that they have committed" (*613 Mitzvot*, 59) and Leviticus 16:29: On Yom Kippur "You shall afflict your souls" (*613 Mitzvot*, 109). These actions do not involve only the confession and the affliction (fasting), respectively; sincere repentance for the sins committed is also an integral element.

Afterword

Techniques for Touching the Transcendent

THE PURPOSE OF THIS book is to shine a light on the power and implications of the transcendent, to demonstrate its presence in Jewish texts throughout the ages, to illustrate that it is our very essence, and to communicate that we have the ability to experience it directly, to enliven it, and, over time, to integrate its wholeness into our daily awareness and actions.

This was my intention in writing this book, rather than recommending particular techniques for meditation or otherwise touching the transcendent. Nevertheless, if I have managed to communicate to you the power and possibilities of the transcendent, it is natural that your next step might be to look for ways to enliven it in your life. I believe that each of us will have to find what meets our own needs. The key is to find a practice whose main objective is to facilitate transcendence. You will know you have found that if, when you practice it, it produces an overall feeling of silence, stillness, relief, or release. You may experience some general sense of joy, overall "knowing," or boundless awareness. The technique will be easy and effortless; there will be no strain involved in its practice, because it is an experience of "going home."

Here is how I suggest going about finding the technique, or practice, that works for you.

- First, if you already have a meditation practice that you like and that is giving you results you are happy with, stick with it. Even if it is not specifically a transcending technique, you may occasionally fall into transcendence anyway (as noted earlier in this book). And even if you don't actually fall into transcendence, the fact that you are happy with the technique means that you are certainly getting some of the benefits of relative calm, perspective on your thoughts and feelings, and/ or immersion in qualities (*middot*) you desire.

- If you do not already have a technique you like, I recommend that you try Transcendental Meditation®.[1] It is a secular meditation technique that facilitates transcending and that has a long history of scientifically validated results. It is readily available across the globe through local centers (www. tm.org) that are consistent in how they teach it. It is easy to learn, easy to do, and has a robust support system for ongoing questions and any other help you might need. I have been practicing this technique for almost fifty years.

- If you don't already have your own practice, and you don't want to try Transcendental Meditation®, then look around to find a technique that feels comfortable to you. Ask your friends and people you trust. Search among the books, apps, yoga studios, meditation centers, and websites that are readily available. Your synagogue likely offers meditation classes. Try one that feels right. Your goals and intuition will guide you.

- Finally, "none of the above" is always a viable and reasonable option. If, after reading this book (or jumping straight to this page), you feel that for whatever reason, meditation is not right for you, then just don't do it!

Some people also wonder about practicing multiple techniques. What if someone is currently practicing one technique (a mindfulness technique, a concentration technique, or a transcending technique) and wants to add another? I recommend approaching this with caution.

---

1. I am not a teacher of Transcendental Meditation® and derive no monetary benefit from people starting Transcendental Meditation®.

- Make sure that you are comfortable enough with the first technique before you start a new one. You don't want to be learning two different techniques at once.

- The practices of these various techniques are significantly different from one another, and they produce different types of benefits. It is important to maintain the integrity of the practice of each technique. This will require patience and discipline.

- Practice each technique fully, as recommended. Don't take shortcuts and "mix and match." For example, if one technique is recommended for half an hour once a day, and another technique is recommended for 20 minutes twice a day, don't practice the first one for 15 minutes and the second for 20 minutes once a day. Give each one its full due.

- If practicing two techniques introduces discomfort or instability, then drop one of them. It is better to be comfortable with one technique than to have difficulty managing two. (And introducing difficulties by adding a second technique might cause you to stop meditating altogether, losing the benefits of the practice you already have.)

There is no one single approach that is right for everyone. Pay attention to what works for you and keep the ultimate goal in mind: connecting with the transcendent, the fundamental oneness that is our essence.

Bibliography

Aaron, Arthur, et al. "The Transcendental Meditation Program in the College Curriculum: A 4-Year Longitudinal Study of Effects on Cognitive and Affective Functioning." *College Student Journal* 15 (1981) 140–46.

Alexander, Charles N., et al. "The Effects of the Transcendental Meditation Program on Cognitive and Behavioral Flexibility, Health, and Longevity in the Elderly: An Experimental Comparison of the Transcendental Meditation Program, Mindfulness Training and Relaxation." In *Scientific Research on Maharishi's Transcendental Meditation and TM-Sidhi Programme, Collected Papers*, edited by Roger Chalmers et al., 4:2295–2312. Seelisberg, Switz.: Maharishi European Research University, 1989.

———. "The Effects of the Transcendental Meditation Technique on Recidivism: A Retrospective Archival Analysis." In *Scientific Research on Maharishi's Transcendental Meditation and TM-Sidhi Programme, Collected Papers*, edited by Roger Chalmers et al., 3:2135–51. Seelisberg, Switz.: Maharishi European Research University, 1989.

———. "Transcendental Meditation, Mindfulness, and Longevity: An Experimental Study with the Elderly." *Journal of Personality and Social Psychology* 57 (1989) 950–64.

———. "Transcendental Meditation, Self-Actualization, and Psychological Health: A Conceptual Overview and Statistical Meta-Analysis." *Journal of Social Behavior and Personality* 6 (1991) 189–247.

Allison, John. "Respiratory Changes during Transcendental Meditation." *The Lancet* 7651 (1970) 833.

Alter, Robert, trans. *The Hebrew Bible: A Translation with Commentary*. New York: Norton, 2019.

Alter, Yehudah Aryeh Leib. *Sefat Emet*. Vol. 1. Mercaz Shapiro: Yeshivat Or Etzion, 2000.

Artson, Bradley Shavit. *God of Becoming and Relationship: The Dynamic Nature of Process Theology*. Nashville: Jewish Lights, 2016.

Bibliography

Banquet, Jean Paul. "EEG and Meditation." *Electroencephalography and Clinical Neurophysiology* 33 (1972) 454.

———. "Spectral Analysis of the EEG in Meditation." *Electroencephalography and Clinical Neurophysiology* 35 (1973) 143–51.

Banquet, Jean Paul, and N. Lesèvre. "Event-Related Potentials in Altered States of Consciousness." *Motivation, Motor and Sensory Process of the Brain, Progress in Brain Research* 54 (1980) 447–53.

Barnes, Vernon A., et al. "Impact of Transcendental Meditation on Mortality in Older African Americans with Hypertension—Eight-Year Follow-Up." *Journal of Social Behavior and Personality* 17 (2005) 201–16.

Bellehsen, Mayer, et al. "A Pilot Randomized Controlled Trial of Transcendental Meditation as Treatment for PTSD." *Journal of Traumatic Stress* 35 (2022) 22–31.

Benson, Herbert, and Robert Keith Wallace. "Decreased Blood Pressure in Hypertensive Subjects Who Practiced Meditation." *Circulation* 45, 46, supp. 2 (1972) 516.

Bevan, Anthony John William, et al. "Endocrine Changes in Relaxation Procedures." *Proceedings of the Endocrine Society of Australia* 19 (1976) 59.

Bleick, Catherine R. "Influence of the Transcendental Meditation Program on Criminal Recidivism." In *Scientific Research on Maharishi's Transcendental Meditation and TM-Sidhi Programme, Collected Papers*, edited by Roger Chalmers et al., 3:2151–58. Seelisberg, Switz.: Maharishi European Research University, 1989.

Borland, Candace, and Garland Landrith III. "Improved Quality of City Life Through the Transcendental Meditation Program: Decreased Crime Rate." In *Scientific Research on the Transcendental Meditation Program, Collected Papers*, edited by David W. Orme-Johnson and John T. Farrow, 1:639–48. Seelisberg, Switz.: Maharishi European Research University, 1977.

Brooks, James S., and Thomas Scarano. "Transcendental Meditation in the Treatment of Post-Vietnam Adjustment." *Journal of Counseling and Development* 64 (1985) 212–15.

Browne, Graeme E., et al. "Improved Mental and Physical Health and Decreased Use of Prescribed and Non-Prescribed Drugs Through the Transcendental Meditation Programme." In *Scientific Research on Maharishi's Transcendental Meditation and TM-Sidhi Programme, Collected Papers*, edited by Roger Chalmers et al., 3:1884–99. Seelisberg, Switz.: Maharishi European Research University, 1989.

Cardozo, Nathan Lopes. "The Perfect Torah versus the Evolving Torah—Part 2." https://www.cardozoacademy.org/reflections/the-perfect-torah-versus-the-evolving-torah-part-2/.

CERN. "Superconductivity." https://home.cern/science/engineering/superconductivity.

Chandler, Howard M., et al. "The Transcendental Meditation Program and Postconventional Self-Development: A 10-Year Longitudinal Study." *Journal of Social Behavior and Personality* 17 (2005) 93–121.

Bibliography

Citron, Naftali. "Carlebach Rabbi Explains the Meaning of the Lecha Dodi Prayer." https://www.algemeiner.com/2013/08/15/carlebach-rabbi-explains-the-meaning-of-the-lecha-dodi-prayer/.

Cooper, David A. *Ecstatic Kabbalah*. Boulder, CO: Sounds True, Inc., 2005. E-book.

———. *God Is a Verb: Kabbalah and the Practice of Mystical Judaism*. New York: Riverhead, 1997.

———. *The Handbook of Jewish Meditation Practices: A Guide to Enriching the Sabbath and Other Days of Your Life*. Woodstock, VT: Jewish Lights, 2000.

Cooper, Michael J., and Maurice M. Aygen. "Effect of Transcendental Meditation on Serum Cholesterol and Blood Pressure." *Harefuah, the Journal of the Israel Medical Association* 95 (1978) 1–2.

Cordovero, Moshe. "Shiur Komah" to Zohar 3:134b.

Cranson, Robert W., et al. "P300 Under Conditions of Temporal Uncertainty and Filter Attenuation: Reduced Latency in Long-Term Practitioners of TM." *Psychophysiology* 27, supp. (1990) S23.

———. "Transcendental Meditation and Improved Performance on Intelligence-Related Measures: A Longitudinal Study." *Personality and Individual Differences* 12 (1991) 1105–16.

Davies, John L., and Charles N. Alexander. "The Maharishi Technology of the Unified Field and Improved Quality of Life in the United States: A Study of the First World Peace Assembly, Amherst, Massachusetts 1979." In *Scientific Research on the Transcendental Meditation and TM-Sidhi Programme, Collected Papers*, edited by Roger Chalmers et al., 4:2549–63. Seelisberg, Switz.: Maharishi European Research University, 1989.

Dillbeck, Michael C. "The Effect of the Transcendental Meditation Technique on Anxiety Level." *Journal of Clinical Psychology* 33 (1977) 1076–78.

Dillbeck, Michael C., et al. "Consciousness as a Field: The Transcendental Meditation and TM-Sidhi Program and Changes in Social Indicators." *Journal of Mind and Behavior* 8 (1987) 67–104.

———. "Longitudinal Effects of the Transcendental Meditation and TM-Sidhi Program on Cognitive Ability and Cognitive Style." *Perceptual and Motor Skills* 62 (1986) 731–38.

———. "The Transcendental Meditation Program and Crime Rate Change in a Sample of Forty-Eight Cities." *Journal of Crime and Justice* 4 (1981) 25–45.

Dixon, Carol A., et al. "Accelerating Cognitive and Self-Development: Longitudinal Studies with Preschool and Elementary School Children." *Journal of Social Behavior and Personality* 17 (2005) 65–91.

Dov Baer ben Abraham of Mezhirech. *Maggid Devarav le-Ya'aqov*. Edited by Rivka Schatz-Uffenheimer. Jerusalem: The Magnus, 1976.

Eisenberg, Ronald L. *The 613 Mitzvot: A Contemporary Guide to the Commandments of Judaism*. Rockville, MD: Schreiber, 2008.

Farrow, John T., and Russell J. Hebert. "Breath Suspension During the Transcendental Meditation Technique." *Psychosomatic Medicine* 44 (1982) 133–53.

Bibliography

Ferguson, Phil C., and John C. Gowan. "TM—Some Preliminary Psychological Findings." *Journal of Humanistic Psychology* 16 (1976) 51–60.

Fisdel, Steven A. "Meditation as Our Own Jacob's Ladder." In *Meditation from the Heart of Judaism: Today's Teachers Share their Practices, Techniques, and Faith*, edited by Avram Davis, 121–30. Woodstock, VT: Jewish Lights, 1999.

———. *The Meditation Practice Within Kabbalah.* N.p.: Katriel, 2014.

———. *Roots and Branches: The Dynamics of Kabbalah's Tree of Life.* Self-published, 2019.

Frankel, Estelle. *The Wisdom of Not Knowing: Discovering a Life of Wonder by Embracing Uncertainty.* Boulder, CO: Shambhala, 2017.

Freeman, Tzvi. "What Is a Mitzvah?" https://www.chabad.org/library/article_cdo/aid/1438516/jewish/Mitzvah.htm.

Friedman, Richard Elliot. *Commentary on the Torah: With a New English Translation and the Hebrew Text.* New York: HarperSanFrancisco, 2001.

Gefen, Nan Fink. *Discovering Jewish Meditation: Instruction and Guidance for Learning and Ancient Spiritual Practice.* 2nd ed. Woodstock, VT: Jewish Lights, 2011.

Gelderloos, Paul, et al. "Cognitive Orientation Toward Positive Values in Advanced Participants of the TM and TM-Sidhi Program." *Perceptual and Motor Skills* 64 (1987) 1003–12.

Gikatilla, Joseph. Gates of Light (*Sha'are Orah*). Translated by Avi Weinstein. San Francisco: HarperCollins, 1994

Glick, Yoel. *Living the Life of Jewish Meditation: A Comprehensive Guide to Practice and Experience.* Woodstock, VT: Jewish Lights, 2014.

———. *Walking the Path of the Jewish Mystic: How to Expand Your Awareness and Transform Your Life.* Woodstock, VT: Jewish Lights, 2015.

Gottlieb, Ephraim. *Ha-Qabbalah be-Khitvei Rabbenu Bahya ben Asher.* Jerusalem: Kiryath Sepher, 1970.

Green, Arthur. *Ehyeh: A Kabbalah for Tomorrow.* Woodstock, VT: Jewish Lights, 2003.

———. *Judaism for the World: Reflections on God, Life, and Love.* New Haven: Yale University Press, 2020.

———. *Radical Judaism: Rethinking God and Tradition.* New Haven: Yale University Press, 2010.

———. *Seek My Face: A Jewish Mystical Theology.* Woodstock, VT: Jewish Lights, 2003.

Greenberg, Irving (Yitz). "The Hebrew Calendar Is the First Commandment." https://www.hadar.org/torah-resource/hebrew-calendar-first-commandment#source-9684.

Griggs, Steven Thomas. "A Preliminary Study into the Effect of Transcendental Meditation on Empathy." In *Scientific Research on Maharishi's Transcendental Meditation and TM-Sidhi Programme, Collected Papers*, edited by Roger Chalmers et al., 2:1051–57. Seelisberg, Switz.: Maharishi European Research University, 1989.

Bibliography

Hammer, Jill. *Return to the Place: The Magic, Meditation, and Mystery of Sefer Yetzirah.* Teaneck, NJ: Ben Yehuda, 2020.

Hanley, Charles Patrick, and James L. Spates. "Transcendental Meditation and Social Psychological Attitudes." *The Journal of Psychology* 99 (1978) 121–27.

Haynes, Christopher T. et al. "The Psychophysiology of Advanced Participants in the Transcendental Meditation Program: Correlations of EEG Coherence, Creativity, H-Reflex Recovery, and Experience of Transcendental Consciousness." In *Scientific Research on the Transcendental Meditation Program, Collected Papers,* edited by David W. Orme-Johnson and John T. Farrow, 1:208–12. Seelisberg, Switz.: Maharishi European Research University Press, 1977.

Hebert, Russell, and D. Lehmann. "Theta Bursts: An EEG Pattern in Normal Subjects Practicing the Transcendental Meditation Technique." *Electroencephalography and Clinical Neurophysiology* 42 (1977) 397–405.

Herron, Robert E., and Stephen L. Hillis. "The Impact of the Transcendental Meditation Program on Government Payments to Physicians in Quebec: An Update." *American Journal of Health Promotion* 14 (2000) 284–91.

Herron, Robert E., et al. "Cost-Effective Hypertension Management: Comparison of Drug Therapies with an Alternative Program." *The American Journal of Managed Care* 2 (1996) 427–37.

Heschel, Abraham Joshua. *Man's Quest for God: Studies in Prayer and Symbolism.* Santa Fe: Aurora, 1998.

———. *Moral Grandeur and Spiritual Audacity: Essays.* Edited by Susannah Heschel. New York: Farrar, Strauss & Giroux, 1996.

Hjelle, Larry A. "Transcendental Meditation and Psychological Health." *Perceptual and Motor Skills* 39 (1974) 623–28.

Holt, William R., et al. "Transcendental Meditation vs Pseudo-Meditation on Visual Choice Reaction Time." *Perceptual and Motor Skills* 46 (1978) 726.

James, William. *The Varieties of Religious Experience: A Study in Human Nature.* New York: Modern Library, 1902.

Jedrczak, Andrew, et al. "The TM-Sidhi Program, Pure Consciousness, Creativity and Intelligence." *The Journal of Creative Behavior* 19 (1985) 270–75.

Jevning, R., et al. "Alterations in Blood Flow During Transcendental Meditation." *Psychophysiology* 13 (1976) 168.

———. "Muscle and Skin Blood Flow and Metabolism During States of Decreased Activation." *Physiology & Behavior* 29 (1982) 343–38.

———. "Plasma Prolactin and Cortisol during Transcendental Meditation." *The Endocrine Society Program 57th Annual Meeting* (June 1975) 257 (abstract). Published in *Scientific Research on the Transcendental Meditation Program, Collected Papers,* edited by David W. Orme-Johnson and John T. Farrow, 1:143–44. Seelisberg, Switz.: Maharishi European Research University Press, 1977

Bibliography

———. "Redistribution of Blood Flow in Acute Hypometabolic Behavior." *American Journal of Physiology* 235 (1978) R89–R92.

Jewish Publication Society of America. *The Holy Scriptures*. Philadelphia: Jewish Publication Society of America, 1935.

Kaplan, Aryeh, trans. *The Bahir*. York Beach, ME: Weiser, 1979.

———. *The Chasidic Masters and Their Teachings*. New York: Moznaim, 1984.

———. *Jewish Meditation, A Practical Guide*. New York: Shocken, 1985.

———. *Meditation and the Bible*. York Beach, ME: Weiser, 1978.

———. *Meditation and Kabbalah*. York Beach, ME: Weiser, 1982.

Kasher, David. "The Hidden Face—Parshat Yayeilech." https://parshanut.com/post/151436866456/the-hidden-face-parshat-yayeilech.

———. "Women of Valor–Parsha Pinchas." https://parshanut.com/post/175592372166/women-of-valor-parshat-pinchas.

Kemmerling, Toni. "Wirkung der transzendentalen Meditation auf den Muskeltonus." *Psychopathometrie* (1978) 437–38.

Kotchabhakdi, Nittaya J., et al. "Improvement of Intelligence, Learning Ability and Moral Judgment through the Practice of the Transcendental Meditation Technique." *Proceedings of the Second Asian Workshop on Child and Adolescent Development*. N.p.: N.p., 1982.

Kushner, Harold. *When Bad Things Happen to Good People*. New York: Avon, 1981.

Kushner, Lawrence. *God Was in This Place & I, i Did Not Know*. Woodstock, VT: Jewish Lights, 2014.

"Lasers: Understanding the Basics." https://www.photonics.com/Articles/Lasers_Understanding_the_Basics/a25161.

Laurie, Gina. "An Investigation into the Changes in Skin Resistance During the Transcendental Meditation Technique." Published in *Scientific Research on the Transcendental Meditation Program, Collected Papers*, edited by David W. Orme-Johnson and John T. Farrow, 1:216–23. Seelisberg, Switz.: Maharishi European Research University Press, 1977.

Levi ben Gershon (the Ralbag). *Milchemat HaShem*. Riva di Trento, 1506.

Levi Yitzak of Berditchev. *Qedushat Levi*. Jerusalem: N.p., 1972.

"A Living Library of Jewish Texts Online." https://www.sefaria.org/Song_of_Songs?tab=contents.

Lucas, Jim. "What Is the Second Law of Thermodynamics?" https://www.livescience.com/50941-second-law-thermodynamics.html.

Maimonides, Moses. *The Guide for the Perplexed*. Translated M. Friedländer. Overland Park, KS: Digireads, 2010.

Marcus, Yosef. "Where Is G-D? Or Where Is G-D Not?" https://www.chabad.org/library/article_cdo/aid/881037/jewish/Where-is-Gd.htm.

Mason, Lynne I., et al. "Electrophysiological Correlates of Higher States of Consciousness During Sleep in Long-Term Practitioners of the Transcendental Meditation Program." *Sleep* 20 (1997) 102–10.

Matt, Daniel C. *Becoming Elijah: Prophet of Transformation*. New Haven: Yale University Press, 2022.

Bibliography

———. *The Essential Kabbalah: The Heart of Jewish Mysticism.* New York: HarperOne, 1995.

———. *God and the Big Bang.* 2nd ed. Woodstock, VT: Jewish Lights, 2016.

———. Online Zohar Course. https://www.danielcmatt.com/zohar-courses. html.

———. *Zohar Annotated and Explained.* Woodstock, VT: Skylight Paths, 2002.

———, trans. *The Zohar: Pritzker Edition.* 12 vols. Stanford: Stanford University Press, 2004.

Me'ir ibn Gabbai. *Derekh Emunah.* Warsaw: N.p., 1850.

Merali, Z. "Quantum 'Spookiness' Passes Toughest Test Yet." *Nature* 525 (2015) 14–15. https://doi.org/10.1038/nature.2015.18255.

Michaelson, Jay. *Everything Is God: The Radical Path of Nondual Judaism.* Boston: Trumpeter, 2009.

My Jewish Learning. "Approaches to Bible Commentary." https://www. myjewishlearning.com/article/jewish-bible-commentary/.

———. "Jewish Messianism." https://www.myjewishlearning.com/article/ jewish-messianism/.

Nader, Tony. *One Unbounded Ocean of Consciousness: Simple Answers to the Big Questions in Life.* Barcelona: Aguilar (Kindle Edition), 2021.

Nidich, Randi J., and Sanford I. Nidich. "An Empirical Study of the Moral Atmosphere at Maharishi International University / University High School." Published in *Scientific Research on Maharishi's Transcendental Meditation and TM-Sidhi Programme, Collected Papers,* edited by Roger Chalmers et al., 4:2407–13. Seelisberg, Switz.: Maharishi European Research University, 1989.

Nidich, Sanford I. "A Study of the Relationship of the Transcendental Meditation Program to Kohlberg's Stages of Moral Reasoning." In *Scientific Research on the Transcendental Meditation Program, Collected Papers,* edited by David W. Orme-Johnson and John T. Farrow, 1:585–93. Seelisberg, Switz.: Maharishi European Research University Press, 1977.

Nidich, Sanford I., and Randi J. Nidich. "The Transcendental Meditation and TM-Sidhi Program and Moral Development." In *Scientific Research on Maharishi's Transcendental Meditation and TM-Sidhi Programme, Collected Papers,* edited by Roger Chalmers et al., 3:2034–37. Seelisberg, Switz.: Maharishi European Research University, 1989.

Nidich, Sanford I., et al. "Effect of the Transcendental Meditation Program on Intellectual Development in Community-Dwelling Older Adults." *Journal of Social Behavior and Personality* 17 (2005) 217–26.

———. "Non-Trauma-Focused Meditation Versus Exposure Therapy in Veterans with Post-Traumatic Stress Disorder: A Randomized Controlled Trial." *The Lancet* 5 (2018) 975–86.

Nystul, Michael S., and Margaret Garde. "Comparison of Self-Concepts of Transcendental Meditators and Nonmeditators." *Psychological Reports* 41 (1977) 303–6.

Bibliography

Orme-Johnson, David W., et al. "An Experimental Analysis of the Application of the Maharishi Technology of the Unified Field in Major World Trouble-Spots: Increased Harmony in International Affairs." In *Scientific Research on Maharishi's Transcendental Meditation and TM-Sidhi Programme, Collected Papers*, edited by Roger Chalmers et al., 4:2532–48. Seelisberg, Switz.: Maharishi European Research University, 1989.

———. "The Influence of the Maharishi Technology of the Unified Field on World Events and Global Social Indicators: The Effects of the Taste of Utopia Assembly." In *Scientific Research on Maharishi's Transcendental Meditation and TM-Sidhi Programme, Collected Papers*, edited by Roger Chalmers et al., 4:2730–62. Seelisberg, Switz.: Maharishi European Research University, 1989.

———. "International Peace Project in the Middle East: The Effects of the Maharishi Technology of the Unified Field." *Journal of Conflict Resolution* 32 (1988) 776–812.

Pearson, Craig. *The Supreme Awakening: Experiences of Enlightenment Throughout Time—And How You Can Cultivate Them*. 2nd ed. Fairfield, IA: Maharishi University of Management Press, 2016.

Reddy, M. Kesav. "The Role of the Transcendental Meditation Programme in the Promotion of Athletic Excellence: Long- and Short-Term Effects and Their Relation to Activation Theory." In *Scientific Research on Maharishi's Transcendental Meditation and TM-Sidhi Programme, Collected Papers*, edited by Roger Chalmers et al., 2:907–49. Seelisberg, Switz.: Maharishi European Research University, 1989.

Reddy, M. Kesav, et al. "The Effects of the Transcendental Meditation Program on Athletic Performance." Published in *Scientific Research on the Transcendental Meditation Program, Collected Papers*, edited by David W. Orme-Johnson and John T. Farrow, 1:346–58. Seelisberg, Switz.: Maharishi European Research University Press, 1977.

Rich, Tracey R. "A List of the 613 Mitzvot (Commandments)." https://www.jewfaq.org/613.htm.

———. "The Name of G-D." https://www.jewfaq.org/name.htm.

Roth, Jeff. *Jewish Meditation Practices for Everyday Life: Awakening Your Heart, Connecting with God*. Woodstock, VT: Jewish Lights, 2009

———. *Me, Myself and God: A Theology of Mindfulness*. Woodstock, VT: Jewish Lights, 2016.

Rouzeré, Anne-Marie, et al. "High Amplitude Fronto-Central Alpha and Theta Activity during the Transcendental Meditation Technique." In *Scientific Research on Maharishi's Transcendental Meditation and TM-Sidhi Programme: Collected Papers*, edited by Roger Chalmers et al., 3:1655–59. Seelisberg, Switz.: Maharishi European Research University, 1989.

Royer, Ann. "The Role of the Transcendental Meditation Technique in Promoting Smoking Cessation: A Longitudinal Study." *Alcoholism Treatment Quarterly* 11 (1994) 221–39.

Bibliography

Russett, Bruce. "Editor's Comment." *Journal of Conflict Resolution* 32 (1988) 773–75.

Sacks, Jonathan. "Righteousness Is Not Leadership." https://www.rabbisacks.org/covenant-conversation/noach/righteousness-is-not-leadership/.

Schechter, Solomon, ed. *Agadat Shir Hashirim*. Cambridge: Deighton, Bell, 1896.

Schneider, Robert H., et al. "Long-Term Effects of Stress Reduction on Mortality in Persons ≥ 55 Years of Age with Systemic Hypertension." *The American Journal of Cardiology* 95 (2005) 1060–64.

Schneider, Sarah. "A Daughter of Tzelafchad Speaks." https://www.chabad.org/library/article_cdo/aid/2222/jewish/A-Daughter-of-Tzelafchad-Speaks.htm.

Schochet, J. Immanuel. "The Messianic Era." https://www.chabad.org/library/article_cdo/aid/100899/jewish/The-Messianic-Era.htm.

Scholem, Gershom. *Major Trends in Jewish Mysticism*. New York: Schocken, 1974.

———. *On the Kabbalah and Its Symbolism*. New York: Schocken, 1965.

———. *On the Mystical Shape of the Godhead:Basic Concepts in the Kabbalah*. New York: Schocken, 1991.

Schwarz, Sid. "The Creation Story and Humanity's Homework." https://www.valleybeitmidrash.org/learning-library/?_sfm_embed_season=2020-2021&_sfm_embed_speaker=Schwarz%2C%20Rabbi%20Sid.

Seeman, William, et al. "Influence of Transcendental Meditation on a Measure of Self-Actualization." *Journal of Counseling Psychology* 19 (1972) 184–87.

Severide, Carl Jacob. "Physiological and Phenomenological Aspects of Transcendental Meditation." In *Scientific Research on the Transcendental Meditation and TM-Sidhi Programme, Collected Papers*, edited by Roger Chalmers et al., 3:1556–84. Seelisberg, Switz.: Maharishi European Research University, 1989.

Shapiro, Rami. *Ecclesiastes: Annotated and Explained*. 2nd ed. Woodstock, VT: SkyLight Paths, 2010.

———. *Tanya, the Masterpiece of Hasidic Wisdom: Selections Annotated and Explained*. Woodstock, VT: SkyLight Paths, 2014.

"The Shema." https://www.chabad.org/library/article_cdo/aid/705353/jewish/The-Shema.htm.

Shivechey HaBaal Shem Tov. Jerusalem: N.p., 1969.

So, Kam-Tim, and David W. Orme-Johnson. "Three Randomized Experiments on the Longitudinal Effects of the Transcendental Meditation Technique on Cognition." *Intelligence* 29 (2001) 419–40.

Soloveitchik, Joseph. *Halakhic Man*. Philadelphia: Jewish Publication Society, 1983.

Spitz, Elie Kaplan. *Does the Soul Survive? A Jewish Journey to Belief in Afterlife, Past Lives and Living with Purpose*. 2nd ed. Woodstock, VT: Jewish Lights, 2015.

Bibliography

Sridevi, K., and P. V. Krishna Rao. "Temporal Effects of Meditation and Personality." *Psychological Studies* 43 (1998) 95–105.

Steinsaltz, Adin. *The Thirteen Petalled Rose*. New York: Basic, 1980.

Stern, Maureen. "The Effects of the Transcendental Meditation Program on Trait Anxiety." Published in *Scientific Research on the Transcendental Meditation Program, Collected Papers*, edited by David W. Orme-Johnson and John T. Farrow, 1:468–69. Seelisberg, Switz.: Maharishi European Research University Press, 1977.

Stewart, Doug. "James Clerk Maxwell." https://www.famousscientists.org/james-clerk-maxwell/.

Subrahmanyam, Sarada, and K. Porkodi. "Neurohumoral Correlates of Transcendental Meditation." *Journal of Biomedicine* 1 (1980) 73–88.

Sutton, Christine. "Electroweak Theory." https://www.britannica.com/science/electroweak-theory.

———. "Higgs Boson." https://www.britannica.com/science/Higgs-boson.

———. "Unified Field Theory." https://www.britannica.com/science/unified-field-theory.

Tjoa, Andra. "Meditation, Neuroticism and Intelligence: A Follow Up." *Behavior: Journal of Psychology* 3 (1975) 167–82.

Toomey, Michael, et al. "The Transcendental Meditation and TM-Sidhi Programme and Reversal of the Aging Process: A Longitudinal Study." In *Scientific Research on the Transcendental Meditation and TM-Sidhi Programme, Collected Papers*, edited by Roger Chalmers et al., 3:1878–84. Seelisberg, Switz.: Maharishi European Research University, 1989.

Travis, Frederick. "Creative Thinking and the Transcendental Meditation Technique." In *Scientific Research on the Transcendental Meditation and TM-Sidhi Programme, Collected Papers*, edited by Roger Chalmers et al., 3:1972–77. Seelisberg, Switz.: Maharishi European Research University, 1989.

———. "Eyes Open and TM EEG Patterns After One Year and Eight Years of TM Practice." *Psychophysiology* 28 (1991) S58 (Abstract).

———. "Transcendental Experiences During Meditation Practice." *Annals of the New York Academy of Sciences* (2013) 1–8.

Travis, Frederick, and Craig Pearson. "Pure Consciousness: Distinct Phenomenological and Physiological Correlates of 'Consciousness Itself.'" *International Journal of Neuroscience* 100 (2000) 77–89.

Travis, Frederick, et al. "Patterns of EEG Coherence, Power and Contingent Negative Variation Characterize the Integration of Transcendental and Waking States." In *Scientific Research on the Transcendental Meditation and TM-Sidhi Programme, Collected Papers*, edited by Michael Dillbeck et al., 4:4661–78. Seelisberg, Switz.: Maharishi European Research University, 1989.

———. "Psychological and Physiological Characteristics of a Proposed Object-Referral/Self-Referral Continuum of Self-Awareness." *Consciousness and Cognition* 13 (2004) 401–20.

Bibliography

Twersky, Isadore. *A Maimonides Reader*. New York: Behrman, 1972.

Verman, Mark. *The History and Varieties of Jewish Meditation*. Northvale, NJ: Aronson, 1996.

Vital, Chaim. "Shaarey Kedushah." Part Four, British Museum, Manuscript #749.

Wallace, Robert Keith. "The Physiological Effects of Transcendental Meditation: A Proposed Fourth Major State of Consciousness." In *Scientific Research on the Transcendental Meditation Program, Collected Papers*, edited by David W. Orme-Johnson and John T. Farrow, 1:43–78. Seelisberg, Switz.: Maharishi European Research University Press, 1977.

Wallace, Robert Keith, and Herbert Benson. "The Physiology of Meditation." *Scientific American* 226 (1972) 84–90.

Wallace, Robert Keith, et al. "The Effects of the Transcendental Meditation and TM-Sidhi Program on the Aging Process." *International Journal of Neuroscience* 16 (1982) 53–58.

———. "Systolic Blood Pressure and Long-Term Practice of the Transcendental Meditation and TM-Sidhi Program: Effects of TM on Systolic Blood Pressure." *Psychosomatic Medicine* 45 (1983) 41–46.

———. "A Wakeful Hypometabolic Physiologic State." *American Journal of Physiology* 221 (1971) 795–99.

Wandhöfer, A., et al. "Shortening of Latencies of Human Auditory Evoked Brain Potentials During the Transcendental Meditation Technique." *Zeitschrift fur Elektroenzephalographie und Elektromyographie EEG-EMG* 7 (1976) 99–103.

Waskow, Arthur. *Or Chadash, New Paths for Shabbat Morning*. Philadelphia: P'nai Or Religious Fellowship, 1987.

Waxman, Debra. "Chanting." *Hashvienu* (podcast), November 7, 2017. https://hashivenu.fireside.fm/4.

Werblowsky, R. J. Zwi, and Geoffrey Wigoder, eds. *The Encyclopedia of the Jewish Religion*. New York: Holt, Rinehart & Winston, 1965.

Wertheimer, Solomon Aaron. *Battei midrashot*. Jerusalem: Ktav-Yad u-Sefer, 1988.

West, Michael A. "Changes in Skin Resistance in Subjects Resting, Reading, Listening to Music, or Practicing the Transcendental Meditation Technique." In *Scientific Research on the Transcendental Meditation Program, Collected Papers*, edited by David W. Orme-Johnson and John T. Farrow, 1:224–29. Seelisberg, Switz.: Maharishi European Research University Press, 1977.

Wiesel, Elie. *Souls on Fire: Portraits and Legends of Hasidic Masters*. Harmondsworth: Penguin, 1972.

Yanklowitz, Shmuly. *Existing Eternally, Existing Tomorrow*. Middletown, DE: N.p., 2015.

Zalman, Shneur. *Torah Or*. N.p.: Vilna, 1899.

Bibliography

Zamarra, John W., et al. "Usefulness of the Transcendental Meditation Program in the Treatment of Patients with Coronary Artery Disease." *American Journal of Cardiology* 77 (1996) 867–70.

Zirkind, Yehudah DovBer. "The Perfect Torah versus the Evolving Torah—Part 3." https://www.cardozoacademy.org/reflections/the-perfect-torah-versus-the-evolving-torah-part-3/.

Zuckier, Shlomo. "A Traditional Jewish Approach to the Problem of Evil." https://www.myjewishlearning.com/article/a-traditional-jewish-approach-to-the-problem-of-evil/.

Index

Index

Fisdel, Steven, 64, 66

Gefen, Nan Fink, 69, 74
Gevurah, xvii, 17
Glick, Yoel, 15–16, 53, 70
Gold, Shefa, 72, 74
Green, Arthur, 13–14, 15–18, 23–24, 28–31, 47, 94–99, 105
Greenberg, Irving/Yitz, 57

Halacha/Halachic, 6, 61, 95
Hammer, Jill, 67–68
Heschel, Abraham Joshua, xxii–xxiii, 9, 27–28, 43, 79, 95
Hitbonenut (Contemplation). *See* Meditation—Contemplation *(Hitbonenut)*.
Hod, xvii, 15, 17, 20
Hoglah. *See* Zelophehad, daughters of.
Holy Spirit. See *Ruach HaKodesh*.

Intention *(Kavanah)*, 9. See also Meditation—Intention *(Kavanah)*
Isaac, 48, 63
Isaiah, 25, 54, 92–93
Itzhaki, Shlomo (Rashi), 3

Jacob, xxii, 48–49
James, William, 82
Jonah, 55

Kabbalah, 13, 20–21
Kabbalists, 39, 42, 104
   See Abulafia, Abraham.
   See Azriel of Gerona.
   See Baal Shem Tov.
   See Caro, Josef.
   See Cooper, David.
   See Fisdel, Steve.
   See Green, Arthur.
   See Luria, Isaac.
   See Matt, Daniel.

   See Scholem, Gershom.
   See Vital, Chaim.
Kaplan, Aryeh, 17, 20, 27, 29–31, 39–42, 49–50, 63–70, 73
Kasher, David, 59, 61
Kavanah (Intention), 9. See also Meditation—Intention *(Kavanah)*
Keter, xvii, 15, 16, 17, 20
Kotzker Rebbe. *See* Mendel, Menachem, of Kotzk.
Kushner, Harold, 98
Kushner, Lawrence, 48, 49

Leiner, Mordechai (the Mei Hashiloach), 107–8
Levi ben Gershon (the Ralbag), 68
Luria, Isaac (the Ari), 21, 65, 73

Machiach. *See* messiah.
Maggid of Mezeritch. *See* Dov Baer.
Mahlah. *See* Zelophehad, daughters of.
Maimonides, Abraham, 68
Maimonides, Moses (Moshe ben Maimon), 3, 31, 71, 97
Malachi, 54
Malchut, xvii, 15, 17, 20
Matt, Daniel, 14, 16–17, 19, 27, 37–38, 41, 46, 53, 98–100, 102–3, 107
Meditation, xix, 8, 42, 47, 63–64, 73–74, 85, 109–10
   Concentration, 69–71, 73, 110
   Contemplation *(Hitbonenut)*, 70–71
   Intention *(Kavanah)*, 71–72
   Isolation *(Hitbodedut)*, 66, 68–69
   Mindfulness, 74, 110
   Music/Chanting/Repetition, 72
   Nullification *(Bitul)*, 66, 68, 73
   Permutations, 67–68
   Transcendental, xix, 76, 110

126

Index

Index

CPSIA information can be obtained
at www.ICGtesting.com
Printed in the USA
JSHW010009200323
39139JS00002B/6

9 781666 758641